Hatch Reflection
poems by
Mary-Helen Leet

*to my friend Mary
from Mary-Helen*

Acknowledgements

I am grateful to my friend Joan Peterson for decades of encouragement. It was she who, when I sent my earliest work to her, said that yes, what I was writing was indeed poetry. To teachers Susan Kelly-Dewitt, Sandy McPherson, Maria Melendez, Hannah Stein.

And I am grateful to several friends. David Robertson whose own work <u>Roads Back Through</u> gave me the format for this book, and who loaned books and advised me on the financial crisis poems, which were initially three times longer. Also to Warren Brownell for books, considerate discussions of this issue, new ideas. Bob Leet and Margaret Olmsted gave me their professional opinions on the financial industry poem as well. Kate Kealani Winter reviewed my Hawaiian punctuation, Mary Dawson and Debbie J. Ward advised on "Mauna Kea Silverswords," and Julie Wilhelm's grammatical expertise informed several of the poems. To Sean Burnison-Lurins I am grateful for many sessions engineering the graphic design for my cover. To Bill Leet, who is the continual tech dragon master, rescuing me often from my computer panics. And to him I am always grateful for abundant polymorphous support, and our shared life in the settings which inspired these poems. *Por tantos desafios que por mi has vencido, serás siempre mi caballero refulgente y querido.*

Thank You to all of you.

cover graphic design by Sean Burnison-Lurins
author photo by Marilyn Gover
cover photo and painting by author

ISBN #978-1470085049
Library of Congress Control #2012916803
April, 2012

For Erica, Bill, and Sean,
all these years.

The mirror of eternity is precisely events in time.
- Victor White

Contents

Preface

Part I- Hatch Reflection

    Hatch Reflection 3
    Mona Lisa 5
    The Pink Cricket 6
    Boat Train 8
    Bayshore 10
    Bright *Thou* 13
    Leafy Sea Dragon 14
    White-Tailed Kites 16
    Scrap Metal 18
    White Pelicans 20
    Pulling Ivy Off The Barn 22
    Forsythia 25
    Laughing With God 26
    Standing Amidst Bats 28
    Evangelist 31
    Crimson Light 32
    Ephemera 33
    Pyramid 34
    The Dad 36
    Bruddaman 38
    Mauna Kea Silverswords 41
    Whale 43

Part II- Tell Them About The Trees

    Tell Them About The Trees 53
    Mayflies 57
    Highway Breakdown 58
    Megalops 61
    Bill 62
    Azure Cloud 64
    Running Through The Forest 65

Elk Lake   67
Warning   68
Denominations   69
Room On The River   70
Rare East Wind   71
Fire Poem   72
Pour Toi   76
Night Marchers   77
Ariadne's Threads   79
April Anniversary Trip   80
Bellevue Triangle   81
July   82
Habitat   83
Jacaranda   84
Hualāla'i Evenings   85
File Drawer   86
Hawaiian Ritual   87
Sunday Night At The Beach   88
Song To The Kalaō'a Moon   89
Dawn Chant   90
Tiki Bay   92
Extinction   93
The Century's Last Full Moon   94
Ancient Species   95
Swimming Upstream   96
Threshold   97
Parrot Fish   98
MRI   100
Short Ones   101
Rain Series   101

Part III- Treading Pu'u O'o

Things To Do In Your Twenties   112
Medieval Garden   114
Preludium   116
William, Cat Burial Poem   120
Forty   122
Burney Creek   123
Owl   125

Pink Moon Descending   127
I-80   128
Treading Pu'u O'o   136
Pu'u Loa Petroglyphs   138
Call Notes From Hakalau   140
Positions   141
Language Arts   142
Puzzle For Sean   144
Aquinas' Logic And MH's   145
DC Poem   146

Part IV- *Mirror Ulua*

Mirror Ulua   162
Gold and Angelfood   164
Salvation Painting   169
Admiral Halsey's Orders   170
Father   171
Right Relation   174
Serpent in the River   176
10-14-80   177
Ghost Pines   180
Meadowlarks   181
Kahakai Huaka'ipo   182
Other   184
Áumākua   185
At Starr's Place   186
Louisa   188
Migration   189
Prayer   190

Part V- *The Eleventh*

The Eleventh   194
To Big To Jail   196
Boat For Sale   199

Part VI- *Notes*

Preface

Especially for all of our grandchildren: Allison, Charlie, Nick, Sean, Henry, Laura, Annie, Niklas, Tina.

Though Charlie, Henry and Annie's names do not appear in any poem, it was their voices announcing their surprise arrival at Elk Lake that made me delightedly drop my clear plastic magenta clipboard onto the grass beside my chair, thereby inspiring "The Pink Cricket." So, you each may still recognize your own presence in this book.

Since the book is very much for all of you who have shared these times and places with me, I want to say something here that may make reading poetry a little more familiar. Poetry can seem obscure at first because it does not communicate directly.

Rather, it presents a state of mind and sensibilities arrived at through the poet's contemplative exploration of an object or issue. *"Poetry is the natural fruit of solitude and meditation. All poetry is of the nature of soliloquy."* It's the sort of record of what you might be thinking alone, perhaps while walking to a friend's house or between classes, riding in a bus or driving up to the mountains.

This contemplative process produces signs along the way in the form of observations, such as the object's similarities to the poet's experiences of other objects or issues. ("The way that branch bends is like how Mom looked reaching into the engine to fix Grandma's car"!) The progress of these images and statements (word hints, really) eventually may bring to the reader's mind some new truth or awareness of feeling.

Without even 'getting' the references implied by the 'funny words' which may not seem to fit quite right, you can still understand the story line of most of the poems and hear a pretty good tale.

And if you read one aloud, you can hear the pleasing rhythms in individual lines that the accented (stronger) syllables make. Especially the lines that have five! Another fun part of a poem is the sounds that the same letters make in a line, whether they're at the beginnings of the words or in the middle.

And reading aloud is also a good way to catch some of the meanings contained in the pauses indicated by a comma, a line end, or a dash. These are the kinds of pauses you'd make talking to a friend to make an emphasis or to imply something you're not saying openly, while being, perhaps, slightly ironic. Pauses slow down the reader, making the meanings easier to understand.

Beyond that, in looking at some of these poems for the first time, you might question why I would have chosen to use a particular word instead of one more expectable. What might have been a more commonly used word? At that point you have some major clues about why the poem was written in the first place, what is its main idea. You can look at those two words and ask how the one in the poem is different, what extra meaning does it have that the other one doesn't give you. Because poets are usually trying to give you a little more than seems to be there at first.

Then when you are reading through the poem, you can pencil a circle around other words or phrases that sound like they might be related to the same clue. And very soon you'll have a pattern of words and ideas that are part of the mystery of a poem.

So there you have it. It can be just that simple. If you're still curious after 'getting the mystery', you can Google a phrase that puzzles you or take a look in the *'Notes'* section to see if there's any more info about it. This section is meant to clarify allusions or references which aren't developed in the text, and is really just intended for readers who might want to have them identified or elaborated. These readers will also probably recognize the little phrases and allusions here and there from Homer, Donne, Dante, Virgil, Shakespeare, Keats, Hopkins, Eliot, Pound, Stevens, Bishop, Thomas, Snyder, Sontag and other modern poets and writers even though they aren't referenced.

Finally, now you can see why I will suggest that you only read a few poems at a time. Poems can feel confusing exactly because there are often several things going on at the same time. They are condensed. Poets are trying to give you as much sound and idea as is possible on just one or two pages. In fact, one of the processes I look forward to in writing is actually erasing words which are unnecessary or distracting from the main idea. So take it easy, just hang loose so you can enjoy them.

MHL April 2012

Part I

Hatch Reflection

Hatch Reflection

Stillness immerses the sky in our lake
        cumulus mounds reach down
              unfurling underwater
        towards basalt boulders glazed tourmaline
        and tufts of pond grass
              gold-green against the mud.
A hatch of mothy alder flies
        quickened with newfound breath and flight
hovers in vertical oscillation
        a rapid two-step dance of up and down,
        hundreds of them just above the water.

Their mirrored image
        penetrates
              the husk-strewn depths
                    from which they've just emerged.
Their pulsing rhythm
        orchestrates
an entire microcosm:
        stringing through apparent clouds
        and insubstantial doubled flies,
ebony polliwogs weave a slow parade
        like black-clad sixties funeral marchers
              crowding boulevards.

True, the leap of any hungry fish
        the thing with scales that parches the beholder
can splinter, unhinge half this metaphysic
        dissolve, deflate, erase our mark
              rend our names to nothing.
Yet somehow joy breaks loose within me
laughter runs her fingers through my mind.
Suppose pindancer angels

      like these flies
         ascending and descending
tap revealing codes
inscribe their signs into our sense,
        signs that still and stir our hearts.

Mona Lisa

Sun's slant being just right
        the trees will mirror her shining
                from the lake's placid face.
The slightest tremor on the water, and
        the pines' skin shivers
rippling across needles
        like flames' fanned waves of light.
Sun's slant being just right
        branches at first blush undulate
              a weltering fever from within
                      that radiates through the stand.
It is then we might notice
        the smile's subtle pinch
              kindling the mind with her secret
of storm sparked blazes
        scorching earth's sere hearth.
As she alludes to the breath of the forest
        we hear her confide, illuminate
                our own contingence as well.

The Pink Cricket

It stepped from under my day-glo Lucite clipboard
        out from the patch of filtered
        sun the color of
        punk rock hair in stage lights.
A nymph who must have been nearly white
        revealed itself in a new instar
fat hind legs and flat-sided head formed as usual
        but pink, pink as bubble gum
        pink as a rubber eraser
        as watermelon tourmaline against the grass.
Slowly he picked his way as though nothing had changed
        through blades and stems, step by step
        like a cat cautious in new snow.

Did he suffer? Did his skin
burn stretching to new shades,
        bathed in luminescence
        intense as blazing certainty?
I did hold him,
        to believe,
watched him crawl over
        between fingers till finally
he stumbled from my hands
        past wildflowers
to disappear into a crevice.
It seemed now he and I were bonded
        my blush over his body
like the geckos and owls
answering my answering them.

Did the rest see it too?
        The red top grass with seed heads
the color of dragonflies,
        the pearly everlasting
        the blue mountain asters who hold

the sky in their hands all summer long.
These lakeside forest creatures
        sistered to one another
could they tell me
        how this happens?
And of this cricket, what did he know
        when he stepped across
        the camouflage threshold into display?
Having basked in florid resplendence
        was consciousness forever elevated
        imagination fused to new accords?

They say the sea turned red
when Kamehameha died.
        Maybe a rise of red pelagic crabs,
        euphausiid shrimps. Or something
greater still.
        In skies off Puakō
a green-tailed comet told me,
        though I could not hear it at the time,
the very moment of my father's call.

I ask to find no gold on the road
        sudden winnings, hidden lover.
It's always there
        the means of transfiguration
earth's will
        to lure, engage, echo
        give notice, warn, steel us
        as we catch new breath,
earth's will
        to elaborate, articulate. To vary.

Boat Train

> *"Whose spirit is this? we said, because we knew*
> *It was the spirit that we sought and knew*
> *That we should ask this often as she sang."*
> Wallace Stevens, <u>The Idea of Order at Key West</u>

Something in their gaze that bears the mark
    of speechless origins
maybe brows pulled a little up
    from inattentive eyes,
three barely school age lanky girls
    have tied together
    all their floating toys.

The eldest paddles a tangerine kayak
her skinny soprano breaks into opening strains
    of a childhood tune, welcome contrast
        to yesterday's boisterous splashing matches,
            polliwog and garter snake catches.
She tows an oblong sailboard base
    bearing a spellbound friend in float queen pose
    whitewater hair that flows across one shoulder.

The fugue is complicated by the youngest
    unschooled as yet in rounds
who counterpoints harmonies of the others
    with high pitched speedy rhythms of her own
and muses from her yellow rubber boat
    on a three foot plastic inner tube
        and chartreuse wakeboard bird that trail behind.

Their chant's intoned as though they're casting back
    retrieving a time before they knew of words
yet what could be the absence
    they look back to?
For it is not the words alone they sing,
    couched now in the arms of the willing water.
Their procession stands in for some desire
    transposed in their archetypal hum

    over the years from earliest paradise
switching for past positions present signals.
They work a change on summer's pageant
    of bathing suits and water play
    of flashy yellows, oranges, lavenders.
Their braided voices recompose,
    ordain the world of objects to accord,
parade before us over the songful water
    images of our own revised containment.

Bayshore

The mudflat shines with shards of sky
        as turbid tidal waters recede
and clay-brown shorebirds cluster
        like a thousand wave-smoothed rocks.
I, too, hunch down, bundled against chill breeze
        amid concrete slabs and asphalt chunks
            from roads and demolitions
                dumped here during the fifties bay fills,
        layered now with drying bottle-green seaweed.
Gulls atop rubber arches,
        tires wedged vertical,
their hoots and hyena laughter
        pierce the kelpy oyster-smelling bay.

The shorebird flock's far edge
        picks up like a picnic cloth.
            It peels from the sand
                circles, emitting continual chick peeps
            resettles, spilling itself along
                the outgoing waterline.
A salt-white egret, wings arched
        into a double bow, skims the surface
            finally pulling forward its trailing legs
                to land.
Nature's archetypal silhouette
        standing starkly brilliant
            staring and stabbing.

A small white cloud begins to
        form and drift across Albany Bay,
            maybe from the factory's steaming chimney
                or smoke from a highway truck
            heading for San Francisco.
But all at once it dissipates, disperses.
        Suddenly it's there again

                    a chemical reaction flashing white
                            but disintegrating
                                    as it hits the air.
Exploding into being once again
            only its outline shifts
                        like fireworks bulging their sequential shapes.
The blossom funnels,
            pours into lengthened vapor streams
                        that speed above the water
                                    then rise into another fanning billow.

Then a flash of bright white light
            as from a mirror catching sun
and all at once I comprehend
            this cloud is formed of bellies, white,
                        as flying shorebirds turn completely over.
A thousand flying as one
            joyriding creature
                        swooping, lengthening, lifting.
Turning their mud-brown backs to face me
            camouflaged, they vanish.
                        All I see is sand. They're gone.
Re-appearing, the cloud's near edge
            abruptly contracts
                        thickens as it approaches water,
                                    and settles each bird along
                                                the new-formed tidal zone.

All the while
            cars stream past small warehouses
                        set into the base of Albany Hill,
                                    that steeply rising strange earth mound,
                        sort their approach
                                    to the freeway interchange.
Caught up in shorebirds' air-built shifts,
                        paroled from demand
                                    I found a freedom undivided,
clarity of form in time, in space

                        motion and speed,
change signifying perhaps
                        nothing,
but beautiful.

"Bright *Thou*
appeared and was gone."
   Martin Buber

1.

I know it's her
I saw them dancing
On the roof
Face each other
Eyes follow, heads turn
As alternating
Side to side
One hops, the other hops
Back and forth
On terra cotta tiles
Proclaiming their bond
Both opposing, and
together.
Now I know it's her
Her paler body
Who's come these years
To the sill looking in
Tilting her head
Different ways
Each eye on me
A long look
Or both eyes
Beak against pane
Till I forgot
Myself.
Then back to
Sunning on hedge tips
Guarding pistache berries
Lawn insects.
How I wish I could
Tell her what her
Silent asking means
To me
All these years.

2.

A few weeks back
A hermit thrush
Studied me
From the glass
Patio table
Held my gaze
A long time
A long time
Then ran right past
Into light blue
plumbago at my side.
He may not
Know it
But I will never
Forget him.
Presence to absence
Absence to presence.

Leafy Sea Dragon

A foot-long yellowed, parchment color ribbon
        of broken looking backward angles,
    a backbone clearly useless to hold
    weight at any point, designed to be
perpetually supported, floated
        sleepily do-with-me-what-you-will dependent
            upon currents of near shore waters,
            not even able like seahorse cousins
                to cling by a slender spit-curl tail.
The fairy wing pectoral fins
    able but to balance, somewhat
and the one-inch glass-clear dorsal fin unseen
    due to constant sculling,
her single achievement being to move
        as rapidly as a whalebone-corseted
        belle in an ankle length bouffant skirt
            would lean from her couch cushion forward
            to pick a petit-four from a gold-rimmed plate.

Inspite of this and the drawback of her face,
    not unlike an eighteen-wheeler's
        square-roofed cab, and the rigid pipemouth
that coughs not fire, but sips what brine shrimp
        happen to pass her way,
inspite of this it is her eyes that hold you
    that quickly shift to look upon your stare.
        And having seen your like before
she slightly tilts, looks at sand
    at grass, shifting focus frequently,
        these eyes her only active feature.

She knows you love her peacock feather leaves
    undulating like lace on slender stems,
        from the little tiara and necklace
        and all along her back and underside,

    long as three pairs of legs and wings would be
    all soft yellow and slightly shadowed in cocoa,
      and many trailing from the tail,
all lilting, lifting with the ocean's breath.
    From under the crown her citrine eyes catch yours,
her drifting draws you back again, and again
      mesmerizing your attention for hours.

White-Tailed Kites

Close-up they've got those
kohl penciled Cleopatra eyes
chin up junior senators posing straight at you.
And the black-belt curved blade beak that cares
only for raiding nests and killing snakes,
death rank emblazoned on shoulder epaulets.

A marsh hawk dives, harries
chases them from their skinny sapling oak
forces them into the rapid ascent
that gives them their name.

One kite hovers
wings up V-shaped, neck arched down
eyes point, legs stretch
drops to earth, lifts off with something stringy.
Against the hold its foot keeps tight to fence post
head winches back, tool beak
stretches out some ropey part
that snaps loose.
Digs again.

On the wetlands path
fur-skinned owl pellets broken open
caskets of acid-cleaned mouse bones,
fang-long scimitar teeth.
From frost-clenched, mud-held tracks
winter's leaden face lifts its gaze
cold bright end-of-winter sky behind
sun-jeweled edges glittering.

Again a V-wing hover, long white
narrow wings, legs stretched.
Another kite passes under, barely missing
frequent cries between them, circling.
Then the first swings out, cuts back

legs out front flies straight at the other
till midair they
clasp talons, spiral
each one wing out, lifting against gravity.
The inside wings touch at center over the feet
the way you used to hold your
friend's hands, lean back toe to toe
and spin squealing, hair flying out behind.

Scrap Metal

Metallic clatter of the fragments'
      staccato clanking at the magnet,
a motor grinds
      the crane cranks up its load
           whine-sliding along a horizontal beam.
The sounds ring through my blood, fur my nerves
      speak their deep words in my skin.
Down clangor and rattle, the rust and shineless clump
      sprinkles in clinking pieces,
the past's throaty resonance
      broadcasts from the crumpled absence of
          a bicycle forsaken, its now bent frame
              unreformed but soon to be, perhaps
      a barbeque or ceiling fan or rebar.

Abrupt expansive silence stretches my senses
      past upslope Berkeley neighborhoods
          to hilltops' grizzled peaks,
and back to these drafty industrial flats where I stand
      looking over the soapy green of the bay
          to San Francisco's bristle of piers and skyline.
This silence sings
      its prelude to reflection
             in some indefinite place inside me.

Not only this realm, these realms,
      not only this space or times between the sounds
placing their presence in waves throughout my flesh
      or drawing me into the spread of silence
          as nearby sound vanishes into past.
But maybe both still and flux press in,
      into this hidden depth in which
three ecstasies of time
      throw me beyond what eyes can see
to the other sides of sight and sound,

in un-nameably spellful merging
       of future with discarded past,
this fluky unmeant marvel of reciprocity
this *wondrous strange* outlandish balance
       of the glittering rhythmic gathering
       of metal through salt-smelling air
             from one pile to another.

White Pelicans
"Nobirdy aviar soar anywing to eagle it."
James Joyce, <u>Finnegan's Wake</u>

Ardent birder that I am, I prize
    my Audubon grocery bag the way
my grandmother saved her large
    City of Paris and White House bags
from shopping trips to Union Square
    when she'd ride on San Francisco's
    Key System electric train.
My bag boasts the American White Pelican
    its long, pouched beak
    pulled back against its breast.
It always reminds me of driving home from the wetlands.
Not so strangely one of our bird walks
    ranges through a wildlife refuge
    created from landfill and wastewater treatment
set miles from town in rice fields along the flyway.

Drifting soundless when you look up
    the pelican group glides
along a circumference about some center
    that only they know,
the black-edged wings not bending at all
they float in silent unison, glowing white.
What you'd looked up for was to find
    inky lines stretched northward,
    the invisibly high flights of Sandhill Cranes
when you heard their
    sticky mewing woodwind pulse
    like pebbles tumbling down
        through a bamboo shaft.

Leaving one morning we spotted a grounded flock
large white birds, their prominent feature
    bellies fatter than Great American Egrets,

     rounder even than Snow Geese.
Maybe White Pelicans or Tundra Swans.
Intrigued, and slipping closer
   we noticed these bellies all
    shook in a delicate rhythm
like tissue paper, or thin white plastic bags.
Yes, thin white plastic grocery bags,
their handles caught
    on dried plant stems
      evenly spaced on the
        dump's sloped wall.

Pulling Ivy Off The Barn
> *"Do we ever know before we enter*
> *which of its imagoes*
> *the abyss will show back to us*
> *when we gaze within?"*
>   Norman MacLean, <u>Young Men and Fire</u>

Three stall, two buggy horse barn flanked
    with wildflowers, grass heads waving maroon.
Ivy spreads the roof with domes
    of creamy blossoms that entice
        springtime monarchs by hundreds
to stop over, replenish
    fanning their tangerine wings in the sun.
Here where wagons once were stored
    my daughter and her friends
    unearthed treasures, imagining
    Ohlone at grinding stones,
at washing holes near the stream on Albany Hill.

Pulling ivy off
    the weather-raised wood grain vine-closed doors
        to get at hand built sections for a stairway
            and skylights I had stored there,
I stumbled into a treasure of my own.
Once inside, an earth dust fragrance
    thick and aged like cold, dry leather
Chianti-ended ivy tendrils
    muscular, tensile when I pulled them
        snapped reptilian at my legs.
They flowed like cherry vapor
    up the stack of coffinesque skylights
    and down as if sucked by instinct
to burrow back out of light
    on their milky bulging underbellies.

From the dark back depths of the peppery air

shafts of sun reach through the shed.
A metal pipe flakes bits of rust
        an earwig crawls around the edge, recoils
                when light hits its chestnut carapace.

Hardened older vines form drapes,
        hang thick between the ceiling boards,
            curve down.
Through cracks the ivy flowers
        sift their continual pollen shower
            catching light
        and setting the air to shimmer
the way that crystals of ice in sunlight sparkle
        after the end of a snowstorm.
These gold dust motes land in the highest cobweb
        beneath which webs from earlier years,
            yard-square scarf sized, pulse.
In late June currents they lift and drop
        like slow breathing.

Decades they've held, gathering specks
        of net-caught ebony pollen dust
till now they resemble black chiffon
        ball gown layers only inches apart,
the bottom edges grained enough
        to show one sooty web edge from another.

Web-locked shiny insect wings
        rise into a ray of sunlight
            cast prismatic spectral flashes
then drop back into shade again
        and softened show their agate lines.
Shriveled blossoms and decomposing petals
        stud the surface of the fabric
foregrounding agitated beetles,
            spheroid spiders translucent as alabaster
        pearls set into crowns
            of peaked high-stepping inch-long legs.

Thudding drums of long-dried trunks,
        thongs of ivy pulled through floor slats
thwang their several decades' resonance,
        back-up bass to soprano rusted hinges.
Images sported by my daughter's
        later eighties rock band buddies–
images meant for venomous defiance
        launched from archetypal webs–
but deeply resplendent as only earth can bring forth.

Forsythia

Their tight ache swells
        splits into welts that
        claw outward, that
blaze lemon petals
        into the year's
        defeated heart.

When anxiety
        casts its blinding caul
remember
        the trade wind fragrance
                of jonquils
        the dusky magma of early tulips
how they fill your
        mind with
        imagination's yearning,
        your blood with faith's hot sprint.

Laughing With God
*The cultivation of the spirit with respect to the absolute,
put side by side with the childish soul, produces humour.*
                S. Kierkegaard, <u>Post Scriptum</u>

Anguishing through Thomist dialectics
        on the nature of God
                of God's right hand
        and God's relation to the world
aroused in me fears of being found wanting
                or worse yet of inflation.

But the little Socratic ironies of the brothers
        already declared to the divine
                are playing with risk
with unwinding the shroud
        of given misconceptions,
with removing idols
        that camouflage, control.

My dream lifts it all into another key
        withdraws me from the constraint of suffering.
Indeed God really is on his throne
        two figures seated beside Him.
And I'm floating up around the ceiling
        that's beamed and muraled
                much like the old library at Cal.
I seem to be asking questions, but God is laughing
        arms widespread
                slipping me onto a different level in play.
I waken laughing too.

Years later we are each allowed
        a brief translated question
and, tolerant, the Thai Forest Monk
        tells me, "All will be as clear

        as that diamond on your hand."
When his helper tells him my reply,
    "Perhaps not as clear as you think,"
the Buddhist master bursts out laughing
      and I feel I've achieved the highest enlightenment.
Hotai, the laughing Buddha,
    marks my garden shrine to my sister
        who so often raised her arms in laughter.

Standing Amidst Bats
It is the part of man to prepare the soul. Proverbs 16:1

Sky as time, expectant,
        catches final tangents
coats the landscape amber
        glazing amazingly everything
then slips off color, fades.

Lakeside lodgepoles shoulder
        branchlets' bushy clumps
        high on scale-barked, rangy trunks
volcano thrown stones at their base.
Evening's last hatch, alder flies
        spread circles on the water.

Wait. Barely audible bells
        their ever present peal
        the high, thin notes of bushtits.
Bird as ritual.
Wait, in prayerful stance.
        I've come for evening vesper bats
to bless me, as when I swim in Kona
        the 'ama'ama part their silver abundance
        or perfect eighth-inch hatchling fishes
cloud my vision. Or the way that
        spinner dolphins can take one by surprise
        early in the surge at Hōnaunau Bay
or skylark voices fill dawn's mind
        awakening at Hakalau.

Patient as alpine perennials.
Bunchgrass flower heads
        blonding like tea-dyed lace,
glorious steeplebushes'
        red-stemmed, nappy, pyramid plumes
open their rose bead clusters

        to flowers fuzzy with stamens.
Anxious as a novice for all those narrow wings'
        speedy beating against a pewter sky
        agile, slaloming through the trees.
Inches close, will they know I'm kin to them
        by stretch of birth, pull of milk
        that heartbeat on our skin?

The moment approaches
dusk's cycle begins to end
        as towers of spiraling pygmy mayflies
        mating between the trunks
        touch their eggs to water.
        More rings. Light gone.
Sacrificially motionless– as though my presence
        could startle bats– I watch
as mosquitoes test my warmth
        dance like devils of doubt
        whine, taunt me as foolish, imagining
bats would come near. Buzz of flies
        sure sign of waste, a lone sandpiper pipes
        its three-note complaint.
Bird as spirit.

Just as I fear they will not come, they do
        ascending on fast beating wings
        yes, these are wings that were their hands.
Dozens cut sharp through unseen clouds
        swooping back and forth
        like toys on rubber tethers
snapping up insects with sudden turns
        silent as sphinx moths,
crossing paths, bisecting arcs
        counter pointing parabolas
the dip, the falling speed, velocity
        calculus of the dividing sky.
Like fireworks coming from all around
        this divine pull draws my entire body,

momentum's upward push
     roller coaster plunge
          joy racing with them through the trees.
I would have been burned at the stake for this.
Pleni sunt coeli et terra gloria tua
Heaven and earth are full of Thy Glory.

                    for Antoninus Wall, OP

Evangelist

Acute March light
    angles off
        windshields, car hoods, concrete walkways
    multiplies into slender steel pins which
        rivet focus
        swell stem tips red
        squeeze chartreuse from branchlets
            pollen from papery
            shocks of rouges, mustards, creams.
The powder cloy of nectar scent, its acrid pinch
    unfolds us
    slips us under the
        membranes that shadow
            our every move
                and hold us back.
Back from Mexico
    mockingbird plucks his hundred
        arpeggios in the ghost pine
    ricochets his embellished chords
        through my mind
            rattles his coins to ransom me.
When I hear him call my name
I want to
    close my eyes
    inhale this newfound
        welcome from the air
    stretch my arms and shimmy,
        jump around
            and break out dancing.

Crimson Light

I woke to see a crimson patch of light
        hanging in the ō'hia grove
transparent over a tan trunk
        hanging fifteen feet above the ferns.
Lying against two pillows, looking down
        through new day's flat haze
I stared in pure perception, un-naming, unknowing
immersed in discovery, in mystery enduring unsolved,
stilling almost as stepping into a hot tub.

This clear color the size of the morning news
a grace note added to the physical world,
        not moving, just there, if you notice.
Direct sun finally clarifies
the stringy mass of an air root clump
that gives the tree the chance of second life
        and in ō'hia are just this lipstick red.
A second life of added grace
        they were for me this morning,
for a few revealing moments indefinable,
engaging carriers, metaphors.

Ephemera

In times like these
        I find myself
        remembering a million
long-tailed mayflies' fleeting
        effervescence, bubbles
rising through
        champagne sundown
or swirling confetti
        or flurry of snow.
Pulled by their
        pheromones into fevered
        clumps, spiraling
upward in their
        quarter-hour emergence.

At times air can
        call out poems to
mother a child lost
        among others.
Or bliss will visit
        the dreaming prisoner
of war, keeping
        breathing coming.

It doesn't matter, the
        shortness of
        beauty's moment, when
the spent silk of our
        wind-scorched bodies touches
        the darkening water, when
our splayed wings seem
        to catch last light.

Pyramid

To feel it, the path between
        great magnets– earth and sun–
this, they said, was Teotihuacán
        a holy place where humans became gods.
But I didn't get the dagger-wielding celebrants
        the bloodied hearts upraised in paintings,
            bloodstained victims.

Climbing ancient steps in earliest sun
        we see thick smog on Mexico City,
recall the wind's swift reclamations
        crumbling frescoes and mural mosaics,
recall men at dawn in dress shirts
        who wait by their eight-foot shacks
            for rides to work.
I'd seen too many gold-leafed altars
        life size Christs, their
sacrificial wounds
        concave with reverent stroking.
And Vietnam, beginning.

Within a few yards of the top
        percussive rock band sounds,
we achieve the summit and see
        we're not alone.
Teenage couple, she chewing gum,
        arise from his leather jacket on the stones
            loosely laughing.
All night long they must have been here.
        My God, is this the only place to...
we exchange glances, I nod
        the briefest of acknowledgments
        and hope they will depart
            leaving this sacred place to those who–

Don't they have any
> idea of the age of this place?
What it might mean to them
> if only they could learn...

But then the fellow leans down
> not to pick his radio up and leave,
>> rather to turn the music even louder.
And he reaches for his girl
> she puts her arms out and begins
>> swaying, rolling back each shoulder.
As he grins and moves his hips
> he drops his head back, facing skyward.
All at once I see they're dancing,
>> arms outspread
>>> sublimely joyous.
My slow smile widens
> as dropping to the ancient stones to sit
> chin in palms, knees supporting elbows
I watch the two of them dance.

The Dad

Parked by sun-glared windows postered
      "SpitFire," "Valvoline," "Screwline"
a road worn, hitch fitted Mercury sedan sat, hood up.
A man bends bicep deep in the engine
his left arm holds
      firmly on the fender
           his sixteen-month-old
           blond and diapered son
who doubles front-over
      to study the sooty motor.
The dad mantalking,
      "Ah...no, we need a bigger
           socket. Here, look."
His free hand clanks about
      in a red metal tool box
      set on the fan shield frame.
Straining against his father's heavy hold
son twists round at a clapping sound
      spike heels on sidewalk
squints to watch a woman
      carrying a shiny auto supply store bag
           past stacked up boxes labeled
"Peak," "Chrome Valve Covers," "Manifold."

Dad ducks under the hood again,
      large, smudged hand spread against crinkling Pampers.
Son reaches down
      catches hold of the keys
           protruding from
                 the dark blue jeans back pocket,
squeals and abruptly jerks up over his head.
"Okay, now,
      just keep hold of those keys
           don't let 'em drop down into this engine,
                fer cryin' out loud,"

and twisting, shoves full weight
            against a creaking wrench,
whistles a tune.
                "Okay, we need the smaller wrench,"
stretches and rattles on another bolt,
son arches back busily sorting
        keys and plaques
                from one side stiffly to another
burbling rapid vowel rich syllables
        repeating exactly his father's intonations.

Grunting, the dad lifts his son
        to one hip,
raises the extracted
        compressor high over his head,
and one foot catching the door wide open
        they disappear inside to talk
                with men about automobile repairs.

Bruddaman

My friend as a child lost both
parents, one in childbirth
the other soon after of a broken heart
then a sister to leukemia
then another brother in a car wreck.
And one more died last Christmas of AIDS.
This death-gentled man cradled a piglet,
    "the size of a five-pound bag of sugar,
two found by a hunter," Ellen said,
    "but someone else got the little girl."
Six months of nights Vince's powerful arms
    held this suckling wrapped
        in Vince's own childhood blanket
to guard against 'pig shock'
    as the vet said some simply die from fear.
Ellen near midnight getting home
    from work at a fine island resort
would carry the piglet up the drive to pee.
Sometimes she'd find Vince snoring,
    Brudda wide awake in his arms,
        but peaceful.
He brought them constant pleasure,
    and they fed him every other hour
        on Snowflake Infant Animal Food.
At six months he spit a baby tooth
    into Ellen's hand.

But now from low where his squinty eyes engage you
    and up the lordly arc of his great black back
        higher, longer than their kitchen table
        armored in shiny hairs stiff as plastic
    and down the rounded, muscled haunch
    source of his burst of speed which sent me
up the nearest ōhi'a tree,
and everyone swore he was smiling,

now all of his three hundred fifty pounds
        balance on pointy hooves
                delicate as any
                        ballerina's toe shoes.
Home from his outdoor roaming he'll place
        front feet up on the second stair
        and wait to be hosed and toweled.

He's a picky eater, won't touch papaya
        likes blueberry yogurt, peas
        fried chicken, ice cream
but every few months will tire of something he's liked.
Last week Ellen came home to find him
        attentively watching a cooking show.
When he wants a walk
        he nudges the shoes that sit by the door,
for a little beer
        he shakes the can recycle bin.
When he's weary he pulls a sheet
        and one of his stuffies
                from a basket to spread in front of the TV set
and Vince will keep a hand
        on the two-foot breathing mound
until Brudda sighs in sleep.
Ellen says if voices are ever raised
he'll run about tossing whatever he reaches
or spin himself in dervish circles, anxious.

Once when a smaller, skinny pig
        approached from the forest
Brudda climbed the nine green stairs
nosed the screen door open
slammed the front door hard
then pushed a kitchen chair
        to reinforce his safety.
How else could one see it?
Seeing it's what the turkeys did
        often in our yard in Kona,

flew up onto the trunk of our car
and fought with the figure in the glass.
        Repeatedly, and often.
Another would throw himself
        spread-winged and screeching
        against a medicine cabinet mirror
              leaned against the edge of the house.

But mirrors are telling, and something happens
        before the beginning of language
for children know it is themselves they see,
        on the whole a human trait.
It was like that the evening Ellen came home
        with some of the lodge's cast off bed sheets
and just for silliness fitted a corner
        over Brudda's ears
        and down his long back like a bride.
He stood when he heard them all laughing,
went straight to the cat
        who'd always purred in Brudda's presence
who looked back now without an answer
        to why he was so much fun.
So Bruddaman did what any one of us might.
He ran down the hall and into the bedroom
and he stood before the full-length mirror
        presumably to figure it out,
what it was about the way he looked
that made them look at him and laugh.

        for Ellen Meader and Vince Dayanan

Mauna Kea Silverswords

Linty to the enticed palm
their fuzzy succulent curved-in spikes
gather light like telescopes' bowed mirrors,
gather light that glows all through
      their own globe bodies,
as diamonds flash it facet to facet
      building fire.
They get hold of Andrómeda's faint luster
sent from the barely visible edge of time,
they capture the fraction sent from first star Venus,
      crescent tonight.
These scimitar clusters of settled light
seem gleaming pools of molten silver
      scattered about the cindered ground
under this gnarled and lichened māmane forest,
those arbor shaped shrubs whose yellow blooms
      sustain the scarlet I'iwi.

This austere land does not prepare us
for how the silver's words speak
      of the air's expanse,
of the clarity like something so obvious
      you should have known it long ago.
Known that the time of the light
      would be impossible to sense
          to feel in your bones
as the air that is impossible to see.
Known that the time, the distance cannot be grasped
when your eyes still tell you
      these stars feel only twice as high
      as you've ever flown in a jet.

How could you
      have followed the sky's expanse
from the great square of Pegasus

>   past Andrómeda
>   up through Cassiopeia,
>   north to Polaris
>   and back to the Pleiades,
> how could you
>   have followed and known from this–
>   this unlooked-for,
>   awestruck grasp of the past–
> that the silver's words will always
>   lie unspied in wait
>   under the cover of nothingness
>   masquerading as invisible.
>
> How could you have known the silverswords
>   would ambush your intuitions
>   open, envelop you, put you in touch
>   with everything else the air is holding,
>   or ever held, or will.
> The silverswords ploughshare our isolation
>   waken us, carry every other's voice,
>   read back to us
>   every possibility,
> alert us to the real we did not see.

Whale
"...to know in what rapt ether sails the world."
Herman Melville

With troll lines spooled from the stretched
wings of her balancing outriggers, she looked
like the archangel Gabriel evangelizing
the salmon to their *undivined final harbor,*
lurching side to side, mowing ocean's pasture
its *tiger-hearted, storm-crossed calms.*
And motoring toward shore
her three masts all drawn upright caught
sun's last light, *flamed like a Trinity candelabra
small on the shuddering expanse of oblivious sea.*
But why would they *fly to the eye of the wind
live unmoored in unpitying infinitude*, this husband
and wife who *slept with unknown shoals
coursing beneath their berth,
wedded by water to contemplation?*

The motor's grumble
could not cloak
a strident shriek
or hide a nearby
buoy's jerk, a fin, the buoy moving north
unfamiliar roiling
something massive sheeting water
churning
then a sudden wrench
a thick, gray, fleshy
curve emerges, thrashes
torment against some
unknown power.
Abruptly
resigned, it blasts
loud breaths,
sprays resounding

harrowed oppression into
encroaching night air.

At once they saw and disbelieved.
Larger than twice their twenty-foot boat
its back lashed round in convolutions
of cable and kelp, as though legend's dread giant squid
entwined its black and suctioning tentacles
about long flukes and underbelly.
What should have been the creature's
most powerful drive,

       the arcing tail, noosed
       to a steel albatross, shrimp trap
       dragged against density's
              hundred miles of ocean swells.

Speechless they stared.
       Colossal entanglement
       mountainous being enmeshed before them
like marble Laocoön's muscled forearm
pressing away constricting serpents
       risen from nether depths against his sons.
For them the light became surreal
       intensified the shadow side, deepened contrasts.
The woman's sudden unbidden thoughts
       of children taunted at school,
her husband's long efforts
       but always something rigged
       hoped for chances netted away, so much
       promised but inaccessible.
She saw his face.
She saw he saw the ocean gazing at them.

He thought of how
these creatures roamed
       the oceans before Adam
that pleaded now

     these centuries past Paradise.
It's bleating cries
    infused into that part of them
that had given milk, paced floors, lifted
    a fallen friend.
This humpback pulled them
    trusting to itself, they thought
"He daunts us, but he draws us."
Up from the soundless abyss of reason
    rose treasure
    some instilled notion
    stilled voice.
Hadn't man-goaled terra firma burned their souls
    drawn them beyond the cardboard mask
    toward some landless high truth?
How could they now
    bear their debt to the
    absolving ocean
that had *smoothed the seams of misery,*
    quelled the elegy within?
Years in the width of the sea the height of the stars
had graced them the forces they still might effect.

On grounds where even a whale's panic's / as deadly as intended assault /
moving verily into darkness / they close the hundred yards between. /
Gradually drifting alongside / they catch the putrid scent of damage.

Tentative she touches
grizzled skin
wary
slides fingers under
the kinked and gyrate plastic rope
lifts
and hears the wince, feels the slip of severed
fat enclose her hand, gripping the tightest
lacerating loop, embedded deep into warm
flesh,
the sensing tail's most delicate

warning flesh
clotted now with blackened blood.

Her face now hot with humanity's violation,
this blood now seeping over her hands
baptizes, re-names them all.
So like them, lungs and warm
blood, milk rich as brie, songs
learned verse by verse, remembered
ocean to ocean year after year.
This resonant mind that reaches across the void,
under this skin and hers
one single salt water river runs through them all.
Through darks that hold
the stars apart blow winds that
plumb the pores of their bones, the folds
between enzyme and blood
nucleus and spinning electron,
emptiness takes hold of emptiness.

The husband pries a kelp knife under rope / saws three swift strokes /
shrill shrieks rip air / the whale's pleated throat arches up /
crashes through surge / throws the sea across the helm. /
Rocking, the vessel finally finds its balance. / Levels.

Chilled with dread
        they stared through each other's
        eyes vacantly into
        the frozen world beyond.
In eddying chaos
        their profound stillness
        awaited the words of the sea
while *doubt*
        tattooed itself to their thoughts
        scolding poor discernment, hubris
sentiment, inflation.

But by some complication

          we re-submit, and when the sea's
          sore spot stretched smooth
          spired its wet breath on them,
the whale also
          found its level and, hesitant
now picture this
          lifts a pectoral fin above
          the side of the boat, then slowly
very slowly, lowers it
          lays it like nothing
          they've ever heard of before
on the boat's
          narrow gunwale.
          And waits. Composed. Patient.
Was this trust?
          Was it hopeful?

Unreasoning, groping intuitively at the bindings
they knelt absorbed to the task
sufficient to what was being asked
humbled
to slip the uncoiled
          serpents into the sea.
          Like Psyche sorting seeds, or pearls
          from the planet's deep-held treasure coffers
they knelt immersed in injury's
          sweet ambergris of compassion.
They knelt like that ancient sandaled presence
          who knelt at a cook-fire by the sea
          to prepare a meal for catchless fishers.

The whale, the wife, the man
          all struggled
          undoing mortal entanglement
threaded their way by night along some
          not-unfolded labyrinthine path
          of cutting, cries, retreats, longed-for returns.

Knowing in its cetacean way / the moment it was delivered from its bonds /
the humpback dove, tested the range of its freedom. /
Dove away, leaving them wet and rocking/

trembling, not
    with exhaustion
    sudden awareness
        of cold that night had
        shrouded about their shoulders
but baffled,
    floated free
        from some coffin weight
emptied
    but infused from the sounded depth.

Then like a song from sleep / that gathers verses through the day /
this being returns yet again / like the Sandaled One to walk beside them /
    one more time.

The hump   the flukes   the rolling wake   and then again
    the head   the rounded back   scallop shallow   dives
inscribe   a wide   circumference   around the boat
    through   points   of their shared   course
together,   as though   the radius   confirmed their
    larger bounds,   devoutly   entering them into
Poseidon's grove,   playing out   earth's theme   of dark
    clarity haloed   around the moon   in a misted sky,
"to know   *in what*   *rapt ether*   *sails the world."*
Coming full   circle   the whale   broke the
rounded unity   wrapped   about them.

    The *uncipherable brow* lifted beside them
        close enough in slow-heaving swells
to focus one eye on the scarred fiberglass hull
        the slanted canopy under three masts
the couple's legs of shiny yellow oilcloth
        the faces, their quieted eyes.
The whale's monstrance eye, wide as
        the spread of a large man's hand

        or a page from the pulpit book,
surely scanned them into some register
held in the sweet, unceasing *watery prairie,*
the *ever-rolling* slumbering, restless sea.

        for Christopher M. Dewees

Part II

Tell Them About The Trees

Tell Them About The Trees

"Tell them about the trees,"
       the tall ōhi'a said
dropping his tarnished coin upon my cheek
as I freed his buried children from vines of fern.

"Tell them about the trees,"
       said the long dead silver hemlock
that soundlessly pressed itself into the trail
       where my young granddaughter and I
          were crouched inspecting scat.
At the only warning sound, a sliding beside me
       something heavy breaking branches
(Bear!) "Run!" we lurched abruptly forward
just as death-stiffed swords of silver limbs
       impaled our place.

Or further down the path
after we'd been praising God with thanks
       a root reached out to clench my foot
       another slammed against my face
and the sight of blood put Laura into shock.
Lying under ice all afternoon
       pondering inflation, grateful knowing
          this is also is how God works.
They tell us something, each of our trees.

Davis Redwood

The redwood my daughter climbed
       to hang garlands of lights
in front of her home next to ours.
       She yelps at stickery branches
while weaving all our Christmases together.

Like me a single mother
    raising an only child,
but now with Bill's prime ribs and Yorkshire puddings.

"Write about the trees," this redwood said
as I pressed my hands against it's hairy bark
to ask that the last
        bits of these ashes
            be taken back into roots
blessing my sister with peace,
peace for her once joyous spirit
        freed into this fog drifted east from the bay.
To ask that her vapors might
        settle against these leaves
        gather onto our grasses
        join into the river.
Her deathbed irony regaled my daughter and me
        in helpless laughter.
After it all her minister told me a story:
Entering Betty's room alone she was greeted,
    "Who's the man in white beside you?"
Only a few, all devout,
        have ever asked, have seen.

Tell Them About The Trees II

Dead Spruce Beside The Cabin

Aimed by another's branches
        to fall exactly where I read each night
its cracking sounds as they changed each year
        told me the immediacy in its will.
So we had it guided by a woodsman
        in the opposite direction
and it fell without a push
        ant-emptied to its center.
And drought weakened, beetle bitten, dead

        the 100-yr lodgepole pines by our lakefront
read back to us our own dilemma
        in rust-brown ribbons that stretch across the forest,
        "The woods decay, the woods decay and fall..."

        Engelmann Spruce
            Father's Day, Elk Lake

        Even if someone–
        not no one–
        is in the forest
            no one
        is who hears it falling.
        Only the crash as it buries
        half its diameter into the road.

In this varied zone of lodgepole, fir, spruce
wedged between zones of majestic
        rust trunked ponderosa and
        higher zone black trunked starry hemlocks,
we watch a sixty-knot wind
        scrape white caps from the tornado-green lake,
listen as lightning spears
        gouge spiral furrows in pines.

Bill sings a campfire ditty I haven't heard him do for years:
        "I eat when I'm hungry
        I drink when I'm dry
        If a tree don't fall on me
        I'll live till I die."
One minute later the lights go out
        and thunder shakes the cabin.
Our eyes meet, "That wasn't thunder."
He goes to look and comes back ashen, wide-eyed,
        "We are really lucky."

The 120 foot Engelmann spruce

snapped its 4 foot diameter trunk
20 feet above the ground
9 feet from where we stood,
drove its limbs deep into earth
        that had fed its roots three centuries,
still its branchlets quivering in the rain.

We figured its 95 fallen feet
        at 50,000 pounds or 25 tons,
measured the propane tank missed by 6 inches,
        the now trapped car by 6 feet.
        "Blessed are You Lord God of all Creation."
That night we opened our 20-yr-old Forman cabernet.
Horace opened wine for friends
        every anniversary of the day
            the falling tree did not end it all,
                and wrote a poem about it.

Mayflies

Mayfly hatchlings powder the lake
        the way particles of dust cling
                to a static charged balloon
                        so light they're blown
            like grains of sand
      in layers over and over each other
as desert winds rebuild the dunes.
These struggling emergents radiate tiny ridges
that pull the cloud reflections out of shape,
        in angular renditions of the sky
              that look like Japanese weavers'
                          woof-drawn ikat
            for indigo placemats or kimonos.
A mist of them lifts gravid from the lake
        like cottonwood seed puffs freed into air,
            hovers, drifts to the forest
        and fertile, returns.
Then dipping towards the water's warming surface
        they lay their eggs in springing bungee rhythms.

Highway Breakdown

Yet again, powerless in risk
    my math mind pulls
backwards to proofs of its own–
      was it always is it will be–
hard star thistles'
    spear-like thorns
        concealed in blooms.
And torpedoing trucks suck out my spirit.

But a turquoise Kenworth
      stopped
and a Paiute of chiefly stature
      stepped down
teeth like trophies of fortitude
Mother Of Us All face.
I cried when he left,
    and straight-backed stared
    dry mouth ghost town.

        2.
An owl flapped
    slowly upward
        over the highway, gone.
Sparse trees
    skinny, staked.
    Strange red fruit.
And actually, a swallowtail.
Then a clumpy
    mothy quivering flight
    of dipping, lifting tans
large and leafy
    over dry thistle heads –
    silent, and alighting–
double winged dragonfly
    glassy, brown-tipped.

And another, like ashes rising,
        flashing its white-tipped wing parentheses.
So, even here the blood rush of discovery.
Scan the landscape
        beauty's movie
        nature's consolation.

        3.

Then mini-market braveries
        at the station the two of us
        pushed the car to.
The mother
        tank top exposing thick burn scars
        her entire upper body,
leans intently towards her teenage daughter
        counsels, correcting choices over something.
And the store clerk, short and cheery
        eyes like puddled sky
stands daylong
        a stone stuck in her kidney tube
        "…a stone the size of four dried peas…"
        in her tiny tube.
But she jokes as she waits
        for the laser truck
        that will come through her town
in two weeks.
"Have a good one, Mr. Miller.
        See ya Wednesday."

        4.

The people
        talk their stories
        as my husband's adding coolant.
He's good at stories. He likes to
        tell of his secret love in high school
        how thirty years later he
wrote me a letter.

We start again
 and, driving, he pulls
         his bare legs back from the heater,
             on full blast to drain off
excess engine heat
         till we find a rebuilt radiator.
My hand on his shoulder
         I hint that maybe
         we can make it
             all the way
to Dunsmuir where we
spent our first entire night together.

Megalops

Blood at the water's edge beside the path
laps unchanged since yesterday
      against submerged mosses.
Closer inspection reveals
pinhead beads suspended in jelly
      consistently equidistant,
a textbook model of crystalline structure.
Bearing a small juice glass
      from a nineteen forties
      pimento cream cheese spread
we superimpose both our reading glasses
to view these measle dots through sunlight.
See, they snap double
      and spring back straight again.
They're crayfish larvae! Megalops,
scavengers in the lakebed shadows,
and next year's feed for trout and river otter.

Bill

Worst that confronts him this year's the dock
sucked into lakeside mud.
Deep in the forest he's always come up with
his own procedures to solve a problem he faces.
Fingers black from outboard grease
he grasps a branchless limb
eyes the foot-long wall stud cuts he's wedged
between our dock and the daemon coupling mud.
With his staff he levers two inches up
jams another piece of lumber under,
hoists the structure housejack-like
then shoves a section of lodgepole pine beneath.

Bill figures it ought to work
to roll the massive weight across the logs,
his tenets being to keep a slow pace
and not to get anxious about it.
Ne pense pas trops, he always says.
Laocoön hours of wrestling logs into place
prying, lifting, mounting, twisting, resting
and trips uphill to gather fallen trees.
Eight rounds finally under each side,
the question is if the muck'll impede their rolling
across the forty foot borders of mud
and keep her from floating out over the waters,
ready partner to our summertime pleasures.

Ramming the rod two feet beneath the dock
he grips the top and thrusts with all his force
against the heavy timber frame.
She groans, and slightly heaves,
the circular log ends' small flat faces
all begin slowly to rotate, logs to roll.
Grimacing a smudgy smile
he shoulders the whole foundation four

then ten inches forward,
eighteen inches– she's sliding free
borne over two feet of mud on the very first shove.

He drops his pole and leaps in triumph
heads for his workshop, two walls hung
with motors, ropes and shelves, a two-handled saw
that Bill and his brother cut cookstove wood with
in their Cascades summers boyhood.
And lifting in orange-brown puffs as Bill strides past
are painted lady butterflies
that drink from the soggy soil.

Azure Cloud

I must tell this to Nick
      the azure cloud that curved and settled
            inches in front of me
                  onto the rosy spirea bushes
the day that almost a hundred
      turquoise damselflies
            blurred the dizzy moment,
till finally I began to count
      wanting to tell him truth.
Stepping slowly past them
      softly they lift
           resettling when I'm gone.
Also about last night
      in our motel room
mayflies gorged green with algae
      so tiny they entered through
           screens and ceiling vents
tickling our midnight skin,
      little ballerinas
           gathered for a final chorus.
A splinter vein of bathroom light
      to lure them from our sleep,
and by morning there they all were
      covering the floor
           like peridot dust
                spilled and powdery,
                      tea ceremony gone awry.
But Nicky says, "There are no
      gross insects.
I love bugs," he told me
      when I sent him a three-inch
           tropical cockroach
               with all its wing sets spread.
"I thought at first it was a butterfly."

Running Through the Forest

Alone on a two lane Cascades mountain road
the pavement slaps my feet
      my chest slams out each breath,
when all at once I'm weightless
      stretched between mirror calls
          of a hermit thrush.
I float from four-note intervals
      through endorphins' oblivion
till anchored again
      by the sequence's minor key reflection.
Again an octave higher
      the phrase repeats
          as the bird's proclamation
shifts to tentative query
      then deeper still to echoing equilibrium.
These high-pitched silvery variations
      string my nerves with silky threads,
draw me into violin spaces
      nebulous realms where distant mists
          envelop birthing stars.

      2.

Bright new stars of hemlocks' spring growth,
      a galaxy clustered about the trunks–
          the forest's daydream
              of last night's skies?
From roadside cinders and shiny obsidian
      glints beckon,
          glass from last year's crash.
Sharp in low lupines
      a shard of chrome
          flashes sun's hot light.
Caught, I kneel to look, and see
      blue sky brush my cheek
          my chest, my arm, my ear–

    an azure alpine butterfly
        teases as if celebrating
            life together,
    summons gratitude for its message
            and a promise to write.

Elk Lake

Near where the spring's creek pours noisily
are golden brown rounded poses,
two deer
heads held steady but for radar ears
that scope the air for clues.
Floating above the pines
a white-faced eagle hunts the lakeside woods
glides against sky, wingtip feathers spread
as children stretch their fingers playing at flight.

Here where the bough tips smoke on sudden gusts
and pollen scums high water marks,
amber curtains of noon-hot haze
blur the hills behind.
A spirit suddenly rises, hovers,
momentary cloud of pollen dust,
drifts into the forest.
Above the ridge three eagles circle.
Sometimes I have to balance
the pierce of it all, add numbers
run a distance, craft some words.

Warning

You know what it's like
    staring at the paragraph,
the red rubber dish drainer
    your one porcelain cereal bowl
        and spoon.
Nothing maneuvers like the tax
    any honor can levy.
I thread through gratitudes,
    blue mountain asters
juncos chipping near my feet
    their young learning to feed.
Chipmunks explore my shoes
    the nearby doorjamb
        gauge my eyes for safety,
perhaps sensing an ancient
    kinship between us.
Grassy relations all around
    three of us species unafraid.
We are not looking
    for the same seeds.

Denominations

Tall mountain grasses'
        lacy sun-bleached heads
stand nodding stiffly in all directions
            with the upright sociability
                  of an after church gathering.
Statuesque but festive
        they unfold and arc for us
            the smile of the wind.

But you're too tall, you say
        for all of that
and want the gusty breeze
        to run his hands
           all over your
              skin, so you will
in the end, abandon your
        ego's little world when he
            twists strong fingers around the
forest's resinous bite, breathes
        on you that burnt sugar taste
            in the smoky heat of midday.

Room on the River

Driving north our windshield frames
      Mt. Shasta's snow-shawled shoulders.
Mounds of white-frothed oleanders
      lace the road. The valley's stately
broadleaf trees are rounded as children's
      drawings of them, their centers
      cool while only the outer leaves
still brightly announce themselves to be
      sun's final resting place this side of night.
Shadows sculpt
      indigo onto undersides
      of piled up clouds.
Breeze forges ripples
      in water-green stripes
          onto the sky blue river
making the surface seem to move
      in two directions at once.
Slowly churning eddies glint
      in yellow light's low slant.

A double sun awakens us next morning.
One rises from the valley's field horizon,
      another reflecting hotly off
          the viscous water's heavy flowing,
          flowing like fresh-made fudge
      pouring from a saucepan.
The air above the river smokes
      with insects' rapid traverses,
and only for moments the surface effervesces,
      flashes like a sparkler on fourth of July
      as more emerging insects break from water
          rising from aquatic transformation
      becoming airborne.

Rare East Wind

East gusts scuff noon sun
      into fiery yellow diamonds
          jutting up from the still water's glassy purple.
Hitting the mountains behind the lake
      the wind swirls back from the west,
advances in broad sheets of gleaming silver
      that move like tidal waves
          steadily over the surface.
A sudden spearhead of air
      stabs the indigo,
          bursts into orange light
like a pool of lit gasoline.

Fire Poem

As though already flooded in flame
        the earth glows *emergency-vest orange*
                between my hurried steps,
forest air radiates a chem lab amber
        under sun filtering smoke
                that dusks half the lake
                      in a snarling mid-morning sunset.
A roar approaches from behind,
        a scolding shoulder-shaking locomotive roar,
a quick shadow broad at my feet
        and overhead, barely missing cone-tipped firs
                the silver bulk of a borate bomber.
"God, they're brave.
Leave.
Now."

Helicopters dip the lake
        200-gallon buckets
prop planes whine, drop jumpers
speaker-cop commands evacuation.
Word's already back this
                may have been set.
I'd known the fear of never finding footholds
        jobless single parent straits,
or later swamped in desk work late into night
        desiring nothing so much as
a place in the woods
        to rest with my daughter. Imagine.
The sign on our road says, "Summer Homes."

Maybe someone frightened from some
        flinty family at each others' throats,
or fired from work, grown ill disposed
                sharp toothed.
Divorced from civility

    sick on smoldering rages
he may have folded venom into his heart
and, smitten, wrapped impassioned arms
     around despair.

We heap our treasures into Carlos'
    barely running Volvo wagon
grab photos, laptop, a painting from
     the outhouse, tools too costly to replace,
    my eight-year quilting project.
Motors, sails and antlers onto docks.
Russian curators packed and hid
    collections of Scythian gold,
     the hundreds of opulent paintings amassed
      by Catherine the Great,
    everything from the Hermitage
carted away in just ten days
    in the face of the unslaked Axis advance.

     2.
Crew base twelve miles
    up the road's a staging zone of fire
trucks tanks tents banks of phones hose
shovels chain saws vans of fighters heading out.
We gather there with other owners,
    ride the chairlift to the top to watch.
Hike from lift to summit in prayer
    sweating even the rote phrases
list trespasses, past resentments
    proposed forgiveness, downright bargains
but retreat to a vinegary *Thy will be done.*
    But, about temptation.
Why do we ask God not to lead us there?
How could that happen, what would
    be the verbs and objects?
Inflate us that
    headstrong headlong breakneck
we'd pray, hopeful of the wrong thing,

        our own conclusion?
              Maybe beg for houses to be saved?
Or God, to draw us near,
may place to our lip too strong a cup
        and, certain we've been forsaken,
mightn't we fall to hopelessness?

Murky opal haze
        mountains an igneous pink,
some unknown off-road
        fountainhead of fire
            deluges the valley,
the flaming torrent cuts new channels
        to lakefronts.
Neighbors stare and someone
wonders what the bright spots are.
And Bill says,
"Cabins."
"Glad your mother didn't have to see this."
"S'pose it's paint makes the smoke so black?"
"Hope they throw the scoundrel into prison."
"Hey, sometimes it's a woman."

In truth, we can all afford
        to lose these get-aways
better loved than any work world house.
Minds finger walls
        for treasures left behind
some reading notes, a wedding valentine
fishing rod in a closet
Bill's mother's bowls
the mouse-holed
        curtains I leave hanging
            anyway because
                she made them,
the stair plank
        more monument than wall
where now three generations have

   scored their height.

    3.
We camp as close to the fire as allowed
next to a river, under the flat
   magenta disk of a moon.
A considerable body
   of fear hallowed salvaged wines
opens our ceremony of sorrows
and we gather slash for
   a campfire strangely permitted
spread Camembert on sourdough
grill chicken, slice tomatoes
eat chocolate.
Carlos pulls his speakers onto the car roof
I plug in Kiri Te Kanawa
   singing *Traviata* on highest
   volume, we who rarely
   make noise in the forest.
Beyond ethics, we sing with her, unsuccumbed
to despair, add operatic *Erie Canal,
Banks of the Ohio*, archetypal
deaths to hide love, *Silver Dagger*'s
   warnings against risk,
rounds of *You Can't Get To Heaven*.
Of that, we've still got photos.

Pour Toi

These years of moonlight
      seeking through the trees
have calmed me. I've followed its glide across the lake
        and down the sky, have come to know–
            in language of presence–
how much of my mind, whether
                salvation or disaster,
it will have been best to never have known.
Larger than human error
      this poet's gold from airy thinness
      arcs up over vermillion gashes of
              what seemed loss,
which after it all tells us
      we have been part of life.

Since the puddle in the path has disappeared
      I've seen now where
        the water snake hides in the dock.
Tufts of duck down float beside me
      a thick and lengthy
        spider strand drifts through air.
And while this cloud of pinhead mayflies
      fusses just above my head,
           a mating scene the very picture
of the buzzing atomic form at the heart of us all,
you may ask why I don't
              flick insects from my skin.
My arms, my face resign to the voice of lack
      and at least I might allow
           these beings their short repose.

Night Marchers

Silence, the sovereign of forest darkness
      by and large balm, can be
the freight train weight of primitive terror
      the cast-iron density of night.
Against the falling of trees
      my fevered indulgences–
           needles pour down
              their harvests of freshness–
are illusion in corridors of dread
              into the end
              of my allotted time,
Athena's shields to shine back Gorgon's head.

        2.

Or whatever it was that kept that bear–
      his large tracks deep in wet sand beside my bag–
from sensing my sleeping form
        sequestered alone on the singing river's edge,
           my pre-Cal Canada kayak trip.
Or kept me fighting the impulse to break camp,
      rescue my daughter–
           she'll call me crazy!–
        from Big Sur's giants' cracking sounds
in the 2am windstorm when she was sixteen.

        3.

But tonight, from the opposite shore's dark pines
a translucent narrow veil lifts
      arcs across the vast moonless dome.
Distinct to every horizon stars by thousands
      reflect in the still black lake,
           its equator of jet velvet mountains
           alone unpierced by stars.
Across this black globe's canopy
        occasional streaks of Perseid's shooting stars

and two slow-moving satellites.
But the planes
    way too high to hear
    too flashy to believe
six of them gliding different ways
        known only by their wing light blinks
            lacing through sky and lake.
The whole thing springs my senses
    takes my breath away
        gives it back again, and again.

Ariadne's Threads

In angled descent
        through morning's side-lit forest
wasps dangle
        trail long legs,
fast circling flies
        zing into focus
        ricochet explosive retreats
            back into oblivion.

Spider threads flash
        gold lights in vertical shade
then fall into nonexistence
        as overhead boughs shift slightly.
Spiders' night work articulates the air,
        tinseled hypotenuses
            link lacy branches
bisected intermittently
        by glitters of dust spot insects, caught.

Not only for hunger has Ariadne's
        measured dance left appraising signs.
Flashing its pastels
        its pinks, greens, gold, white,
this geometry of spectral beams
        gleams loomed grooves,
            sings her concentric hymn,
                a tale of life's order.

But, backtracking we see that
        these redwoods also stand in circles
            of ever widening diameters
sprung from the graves of ancestors,
        the man-sawn moss-felted
            table size stumps
their mournful markers
        bearing dreadful elegies.

April Anniversary Trip

Wild river bursts off the unreal
hulking cliff's carved rim
lifts out, shatters into banks of mist
and pitches headlong, roaring
past the sun-bleached looking granite face,
colliding into the pool below
crashing all night long.
Camped near the falls is like sleeping
at the airport with windows open,
jets revving engines toward their gates,
or living by the freeway's steady rush.
Except of course for the fragrances
of humus thawing into snowmelt
pine breathed in from overhead and underfoot,
and the white drapery of water
falling from that impossible height.
Chill of grilling fish in early dark,
a visit from the only other campers
had we heard there could be heavy flooding?
Then many blankets over us, knit caps.
Yosemite Creek slips past
under wind-ploughed boughs.
After fifteen years we take freeways
in our stride. Like a lot of things.

Bellevue Triangle

Sunlight caught in symmetry
    of upright fleshy yellow feathers–
barley drying, standing ripe
    translucent as honey
and gravid as gold with safety's promise
    for those who ply these lands.
Out of the orange and magenta hills
    a dust spot screeches through violet haze
enlarges, expands, advances, becoming
    a throbbing flock of geese, yodeling and barking.
Their undersides glow in sunset like molten iron,
passing low to land on some rancher's pond
    where slate-blue sculpted mountains meet
        the fresh cut green alfalfa.
The gridlock of their shouted recitative
    congests the air that fans upon us
        their bracing resolve.
They humble us, laboring into night
    their forceful wings throwing flame.

for Jim Baldwin
Kenny Schoessler
Rocky Sherbine

July

Impossible this,
    to write about fireflies,
        and children leaping
           all about in dusk.
Soundless blink
    of green fluorescence
there, near
    coaxing my blossomed mind
        to everywhere.
Playing run to Grandma
    two on my lap in the grass
after a movie and backyard baseball.
Stories in bed
    when you were a girl
        forties history, lightning.
Asleep like cloth dolls
    in un-inventable poses
        still as museum treasures.

Habitat

Compulsively counting
        thirteen wild turkeys in our yard,
a half-dozen chartreuse chameleons
                on my railings.
Or staring
        suddenly I realize
            realize the trees above
                are filled with butterflies.
They float
        from tree to bush
           and back
                drift, glide, tilting their silver
                      orange and black.
They shouldn't surprise me,
        I planted crown flowers
        and lilikoi vines
                to draw them to us.
But seeing them makes my chest contract
        and my body warms as though
                it's still the first time.

Jacaranda

Breeze blown sky-blue jacaranda blossoms
pelt the aqua quilt
I'm sewing ocean fishes in
to celebrate "my only first granddaughter's"
courage to keep her face mask underwater
to see the lavender corals in turquoise rooms
to discover the ocean's world.
Hawk-like we glide over the reef
our eyes intently follow creatures,
strive to memorize their glory
set their proportioned balances
as standard to our lives.
(And, yes, the joy here buckles near our hearts).

Stitching in lines of waves
thinking of what her life is like,
her made up phrases
joys of ōhelo berry picking
invented play with neighbor Kealy
weary children sighing into their milk glasses.
Spiraling calls of ring neck doves
embroider ringlets of sound
into the sea-blue afternoon
while through the pattern a three-inch white-eye warbler
threads trills and trebles.
And a hundred honeybees' glorious hum
swells the canopy above.
Every year this fallen carpet of violet blooms
settles my body into my soul.

Hualāla'i Evenings

Sunset, and roadside power lines gleam magenta.
Saffron finches settle in
    and monarchs alight to hang like
        jacaranda seedpods all night long.
Final rays obscure lava ridges
volcanic knolls darken in chill mists.
Lingering, the moon ascends
    magnetically intimate
        attendant as a lover.

Husky hapa-Hawaiian man
strides to the bandstand
    musicians' request
to grace their audience with dance.
Obliging, still in work clothes– Levi's, boots
    rodeo prize silver buckle.
Smiling, he listens for opening bars
    and dropping his knees slightly,
        steps into a fast-paced *paniolo* hula.

    II.
Koas stretch thick tufts
    apricot with sunset
into the sway of evening winds
    like a young *kahiko* dancer
shaking her hair about her shoulders.
As upland breezes balance their differences
    currents gather round our campfire
        warming themselves.
Smoke reaches, caressing stilled tresses
    settles his stately forest companion
        into night's depth.

File Drawer

Soon to be leaves and coffee berries
her words black now
like the rodeo's bucking bull
named Lawsuit.
Blood glow under campfire ash
like Pele's heart in Halema'uma'u Crater.
Sunset peach in cindering clouds
downslope houselights of our hillside
candles on our glass top table.
Lonely, remembering
    three white leopards
      bones glad to be parted.
Each night the planets shift
    the Cross scribes its arc
      and the new moon edges to full.
Silver stray
    stretched asleep beside me.
My daughter and her son
may come for Christmas.

Hawaiian Ritual

Every New Year
        hundred-foot chains
                of red firecrackers
drape from front lawn
        scaffolds
        or rope thrown over a limb.
Non-stop fireworks
        roar across midnight hillsides
screeching folks' exuberance
        release from yearlong overtime,
                second jobs.
Spheroid shards of sparks boom
        through smoke drifts,
whoops and cheers of
        Hau'oli Makahiki Hou!
        Waydu go, bruddah!
        Maika'i!
connect our homes *mauka* and *makai*
        sing us the size of our neighborhood.
Laughter
        nets us yard by yard for days
        rewards the largest paper piles
while winter runoff washes powders
        down through aquifers,
seeps up through the reef.

Sunday Night at the Beach

From domed shore-tree silhouettes
      dark shapes move noiselessly
carry sleeping children
      ice chests, all the equipment of leisure.
Stinging from exposure
      swathed in aromas
          of dissipated barbeque
          and ocean salt
they make their way
      toward the wall of cars.
All down the line
      in the voiceless black
motors start up, idle.
      Doors close.
White lights stream slowly
      toward Hualāla'i
      toward dim stars of upslope homes
softened under her blanket of cloud.

Song To The Kalaō'a Moon

Again the certainty of her midnight apex
blazes white off hard surfaces.
Beacon of reliability
continuity made visible
creator of history, cycling expectations.
Often the full moon's penetrating stare
through our open window
wakes me and I'll stand outside and
face her, high and solitary.
Her unwavering shield of widened roundness
calms my arms, feet, mind
bolds me bright
against the claws of chance.

Dawn Chant

Daylight has pierced
      a small bright stain
           into the clouded horizon.
White robed monks
      have spaced themselves
           in forest clearings,
question and answer calls
      of nightingales and cardinals
           fill the valley.
Crickets purring, dove *ahems*
      occasional peacock cries of *help!*
           And something else.

Focused by blinding green corridors
      twelve-foot coffee trees
           lush to the ground
                like Christmas.
Lift, place, incense, camphor, breathing
      remember
           remembering
candles mirrored in shining gold
      blossoms, blossoms
           little bells
                hearing.

Racket of nervy mynahs
      finally ceases messing daybreak sounds
and finches' squeaky roll begins,
      builds reverberations deep within
like one long, warm insistent sigh
      from the monks' iron singing bowl.

Remembering
      upright mounds of saffron robes
           how their sonar chant

                bores into my bones.
Hearing, listen, listening
        the wind's approach
                rustles nearby branches.
The webbed air is ionized
        wired across the canyon
                by currents of living sounds.
Punctuating silences
        shape the chant of the land.

Tiki Bay

The stretched waves surge to shore
        their volume swells and smashes against the seawall.
Palm frond shadows
        move with the speed of wind
                like great lizards chasing
                      over sundown's yolky stones.
Mornings we sit on the wall
        dropping bits to entice eels up,
                writhing over rocks and one another
                      making do with tight, joined spaces
                              within the lava's weighty mass.
These waves' insistent rumble, their scratchy retreat
        make me more real, substantial
                having watched them, heard them
                lain next to them listening all through sleep.

                                      for Duane and Marjorie Erway

Extinction

A single cardinal
        signals in morning moonlight
and soon an entire hive of wild bees
            resonates busily
in the sixty foot mass of eucalyptus blossoms
              fuzzy, greenish white,
the smooth-skinned trunk of pinks and acrid greens
          worthy of Monet, Vuillard.
Every branchlet rocks in breeze
        as the feverish seethe
              of tremulous specks shivers,
erases the night from each cluster.
        What would we be without them–
            blossom brushers, tassle shakers.
        Or, would we even be?

Backlit by daybreak
        its creamy Mauna Kea silhouette
breathes new air
        into the freeways of bees
            and dozens of butterflies.
Tweaky pronouncements
        of chattering finches and warblers
have replaced the daylong songs
        of the cardinal flock
from the time before the lot below
        was cleared of Christmas berry trees.

for a rare painted bark eucalyptus cut down to make a view

The Century's Last Full Moon

Decades stretch across my mind
    ricochet off the moon's roundness.
Fibrous white turnip
    separation dream
        staring into 1970's New Year's moon.
Tonight's snowy cavity
    of contracted coconut
        her plentitude evaporated.
Could my lifelong spreading pain
    now nourish koa and ōhi'a
        that apapane might sing?
Without this forge of linkages
    who will I be?
Is a poem enough?
    Breeze touched slope
        of possibility
could the full moon
    be enough?

Ancient Species

Through leggy yellow impatiens stems
        sleek leaves and white, five-petal
            ruby-center flowers
your pale, long jaw line lies against
      the burnt sienna hand turned crock's flat rim,
curving the pot's edge from nose tip, throat, along belly
      through exquisite length of tail,
          your long toes grasp the sides.
Perfectly still, a half closed eye looks into mine.
You, can you
      can you imagine
          how comforting is
              your gaze upon me
                  your gaze upon me?
You turn back to look
      after hunting abit
      you even gaze down from
          a nearby bare plumeria branch,
      extend your pink throat disc
        in regal declaration,
           eyeing me again.
Just when I needed you.

for Ryan Alfonso

Swimming Upstream

Saffron finch fledglings
bathe in drenched leaves.
Swimming upstream
    they leap arched
        feathery rapids,
the ferny leaves of our royal poinciana,
    flashing lemon bright spots
        relinquishing camouflage.
And like blue-lipped shivering children
        unwilling to leave the pool
they return for more– despite
    the threatened retreat of parents–
        exuberant even in exhaustion.

Threshold

At ocean's edge you can
        see the earth breathing.
The sea slides its glass fingers
        along land's coral-pebbled skin.
If the clear water rises
        to rocks on which you sit
the sands of her breast will swell
            and inhale, magnify
then release with a sigh
        as waters recede.
Too, through clear air
I have seen across the valley
        a mountainside throb
as I crested the ridge
        my blood fast with climbing.

Parrot Fish

Train trip chat of wetland species
recent travels, news of children
our husbands' companionable traits
and how as couples we've been musing
on death's no longer distant approach.
Crossing a plaza to catch a bus
we strolled the open air market
morels, chanterelles, endives
plums in yellows, reds and greens
fish flown fresh from many Pacific waters,
a heavy-fleshed *Uhu* seen in Hawaii's
finest cuisines.
Throughout the day I dreamed up
recipes for a party with my daughter.

Outside the de Young we shared prociutto
chevre, fruits, and Belgian chocolates.
And inside admired the several types of light
on Monet's flock of white turkeys,
chartreuse reflected onto chests from grass
yellow from sun direct on backs
and gold glowing through the backlit tails,
spread, with even a bit of rose
cast from Monet's big pink house.

Back at home a visit with my neighbor
phone calls, mail, chores
and finally rinsing and wrapping the fish for the night.
As though alive it slid in my hands
from the turquoise tail to its coral scraping tooth
the wide beak that scared me from the water
first time I saw one in Hanauma Bay.
The large-muscled reef swimmer body,
its overlapping coins of armor

still transparent, shielding yellow skin
swathed with turquoise and bright green,
shading around the face to pink like Peace, the rose
the startling pink that astounds us
when we swim near, honored it's not afraid.

Above the flat, round cheek that covers gills
are radiating asterisk eyelash lines
that draw one's gaze into its own,
and even as it slipped about in my hands
I looked back into the gray, darkened eye
and then my tears welled up and I could not stop
and I said I was sorry, sorry about us all
but still I could not stop
till after I'd covered it with roses
and buried it in my garden, deep where nothing
could get at it ever again.
And I knew that this was one more of those things
my friend and I were talking about,
no longer heedless of time's flight.
A thing I'm all at once aware I'll never do again.

MRI

Nobody told me the little men would come
and a woman's clear voice as well.
Cross-eyed close in this vinyl tube
airliner recessed lights
edges press my arms too tight
so I clasp my hands across my chest
and struggle to dispel the coffin lid.
She asks, "Are you all right?" "Of course."
Of course. But nothing shields out the loud
banging you've all heard about, coming at you
in rapid fire shots, horns and wrong turn buzzers
for longer than supplication can hold,
longer than any plan the mind could give.
Insistent unwanted intimacy
hornets of sound send their buzzing
needles through my crippled tissues.
Lower pitch drumming answers
in a rhythm intricate and speedy.
From behind my ear a nose flute whines.
Then I know it's all right,
they're talking through my body
these shaman dancers from sere but hopeful realms.
All around me they are dancing
high-stepping in white wrapped leggings
eyes pierce out from coal black rings on chalk face,
white and black head feathers point flat out.
"Their headman's cow-horned death's-head"
chants from the chest, and all of them
aim their minds into my injured spine
each beating with stick or hand
their own peculiar sine wave through me.
Generations they've sung this song of healing,
their prayers pass through my circled body,
and finally I am sorry when the sounding ends.
       for Denyse Nishio

Short Ones

Rain Series
Wonderful, that so much water
is breaking out from the clouds,
which do not have any solidity.

I.
Hailstones in the Freezer

Announcing itself with
crackles, splats, claps on concrete doorstep
and gongs on a covered tin bucket,
the fat-fingered rain strums its hollow
thonks on the cedar-shake wood shed roof
like a one-note bamboo wood chime.
The storm stammers on the metal roof of our cabin
and in a not so eloquent rush
comes out with it in open vowels
full-on diphthongs, having his boasty
say in a Sawtooth Stanley Basin drawl
droning on about "a cow peein' on a flat rock."
Suddenly, it batters loud like the roof has thrown a rod
and thousands of foot-high spikes
shoot up from the lake.
The one-inch hailstones I saved for neighbors to see.

II.
Kalāo'a

In phrases heavy laden with intent
the unyielding sky pours forth its fluent soliloquy
speaks its mind through silver-tongued needles in street lights
their frosty sodium vapor orange
dissolves in the rain-pocked sheet of blown wavelets
sliding down the drive's spillway,
and somehow I can't help feeling it says I'm rich.

III.

The pregnant air cloys, blurs white
luxuriates, flaunts her opulent
gleam in the lavishing porch light,
flourishes rain's beamy lace drapery
twirling across the grass
with splashy maternity that swells soil
fills every cavity, anchors, settles
leaving no emptiness.

Where it folds, the roof throws off
a talkative rivulet
cascades its shaky falsetto
clapping onto lava pebbles
an effusive babble of speedy consonants
splashing on stones in Ts, Ds, Ss.
A high-pitched sound like paper slowly tearing
is the constant static from wet power lines.

A chorus of many raindrops rattles
on passion fruit leaves as three-year old Allison
reaches fingers into the run-off.
I go to get a glass to catch it in
and hear, "Wait for Grandma, rain."

IV.
Volcano Rainforest

Clouds throw themselves
at our feet
feasting us, lush treats
violets, orchids
camellias, azaleas.
On the porch swing
we sip tea and cocoa
awaiting any small break
in the wind driven downpour
to hear apapane, ōma'o. *for Joann Morse*

V.
Hula Kalāo'a Mauka

The moon is full, the wind at last
has blown the storm beyond our sky.
The trees are still, the air is soft
and flowers soon will return
perfumes to our land.
The pounding of the gusty winds,
strained trees and restless sleep
and downpours soaking through the screens
have shut us in our thin-walled house.
At last the breeze will waft through rooms,
and sitting at our desks we'll hear
birds cheering from our yard again
and our souls extending into silences.

Epiphany

The week after Christmas
dawn's brief light came in horizontal
    just under a heavy cloud layer
catching three levels of green plastic ties
    backlit and glowing
        like New Year's traffic signals
in the dark field of dormant trees
    in the new orchard.

Creekbank

    Sometimes even
a flattened streamside wreck
will glisten Burmese-ruby red
    in early sun refracted
        through raindrops that veil
its scarred and faded paint.

My Father's Japanese Maple

Sunlight shines up briefly
    through the lowest
        of her branches
bright a moment, crimson glowing
    stretching finger leaflets.
Chilling now, and muter grow
    the shadows at her heart.
Dark takes over, night descends
    and autumn turns to death.

Parasite

Never before seen
heavy, black-bellied yellow jackets
     going into our dead box elder,
and the trunk emitting
     frequent puffs of wood dust.

Turned out they were wasps
carrying black house flies
     into holes in the tree.
They lay eggs in the flies,
which then become feed
     for young wasps.

Thief

Harvesting wildflowers
For an engagement card.
The mosquitoes know
They've got me now
Hands busy
Heart exuding guilt.

Hapuna

Jelly clear green glass wave
     curling back under me, water
          tunnels dark pulling me nearer
               beauty's compelling embrace.
Crashing light sparkles life's substance
     blinding resistance to see,
          loosens, releases these bindings
               sinking, I'm rising to Thee.

Valentine for Bill

Second hand McDonald's toy
proudly smiling chartreuse Kermit
hands securing her waist over his head.
Pink-clad Miss Piggy
proud snout high
tongue-showing smile,
arms in flight position
fingers stiffly skyward.
Push the little turquoise base across a tabletop
the frog does Nureyev pirouettes
displaying Piggy's perfect extensions,
her eyes closed in ecstasy.

At George's

Black modeled fox
lopes along lawn edge
past white birch bark
pausing, preying
fish sleek
tail tipped glacier white.
Dusk at Snow Creek.

At Elk Lake

The golden mantle ground squirrel
comes out to settle inches away
while we break our peanuts open in the sun.
He digs in needles near our feet
to nibble treasures from the stores
we saw him hiding last September.

White Flecks

Sift down.
A needle, black
Settles on
My arm.
Flicked, it only
Smudges.

Black and Spikey Skeletons

There is no light like the
air thick as honey
thick as the knowledge
of death
soft on the lumpy
bed of needles
blurring shadow edges.
Nothing looks like the flat disk
of blue-red blood of kings
that is the sun
inlaid in the stone white sky
soaking into barks
that moments ago were centuries old
titans breathing, sucking the river
of life from the soil.
Their bodies, now dense in the air,
shroud the mountain on which
they no longer stand.

Reclaim

Time, water, winter
       relax downed trees
conform them
press, suck, slink them
as soil clings to curved
       volcanic surges
              of earth's earliest spine.

Part III

Treading Pu'u O'o

Things To Do In Your Twenties

Marry a man who'll talk back to your mother.
Do it on your 20th birthday.
Camp at the top of Mt. Diablo.
Gather twigs and two rocks for a cook fire.
Watch the clouds turn pink below you.
Learn to cook while he reads history to you.
Make him shirts.
Make sour milk pancakes every Saturday morning.
Follow with strolls in Tilden Park.
Go to free museums every Sunday.
Walk on Ocean Beach.
Dig with your fingers in crumbly dirt.
Breathe in its leaf mold smell.
Backpack to a frozen alpine lake
when your doctor thinks it's Hodgkin's.
Study theology with the brothers.
Sit on back stairs in morning sun.
Inhale the smoky tea steam through your nose.
Let the finch song reach into your bones.
Let flowering onion and sour grass grow in your lawn.
Hang your paintings in the garden.
Propagate everything from cuttings.
Nail boards on window sills for bird seed.
Prepare quenelles every night till they're perfect.
Quit using birth control, throw up for nine months straight.
Hold your newborn daughter all day long.
Baptize her yourselves in Ocean Beach's layered waves.
Write a storybook to read her.
Go barefoot.
Play the new rock. Dance.
Drive to Sonoma with other mothers to harvest figs.
Bring home cherry cider.
Invent avocado and fig ice creams.
Read all of Susan Sontag.

Begin analysis when Bobby Kennedy dies.
Counsel new mothers. Start a play group.
Let the children go naked in the sun.
Go to SDS and New Mobe meetings.
Hold weekly letter writing brunches.
Stand in front of the National Guard's lowered bayonets.
Fear arrest.
Fight with your husband about the war.
Divorce.
Tell Alice No, you can't start a restaurant with her.
Set up a family day care home, go to school at night.
Quit cutting your hair.
Walk alone to the waterfall at Fallen Leaf.
Keep on walking all day to Desolation Valley.
Walk back down and break up with your lover.

Medieval Garden

Manuscripts rich with oranges
pearls and lapis skies
painted in 14th century monasteries,
I too was formed in solitude
and saved from early nihilists
by poetry and microcosms, gold to airy thinness beat.
And so much more I had not seen would matter.
Freedom to try guided by
a cowboy six-foot-five,
abstract painter who motorcycled
two hours through fog to meet at 8am.
Delighted with my paintings
he skipped across the central quad
leaving forty yards of boot prints
crunched into the hoary frozen lawn.

Upcountry year of daily studies
book lined yellow room
windows like Chinese scrolls
of rain-black age gnarled branches
blossom embellished
then nephrite leaves and finally
apricots fat as friars on donkeys
riding with lush-robed nobles on pilgrimage.

Next year rocking my baby in predawn chill.
Ardent steady sucking sounds
and frequent restful sighs,
her sustained hum rising five notes,
a purring, up-note glissando
her hand against her cheek
fingers curled, then stretching slightly.

As skyline forms against the stars,
roofs appear and flowers shape.

Birds begin with tentative chips
a sparrow's single piercing tests the dawn,
robins' steady *cheer-roops* confirm
that soon the light will crest the hills.

My daughter's sweet, milk-smelling hair
her sleeping head moves down and up with every breath
her belly presses up against my arm.
Inquisitive eyebrows arch over
silky domed lids that arc curved lashes
onto powder soft rounded cheeks.
Mouth a perfect oh lightly taking in
then emphatically exhaling,
sighing the cycle to completion.
Greens stand out and morning fills
with red-chested finches' fervent anthems,
the horizon line electrifies
polarizes earth and sky.

And then to hear about the war
mothers receiving folded flags
crisply lifted from sons' coffins
fruit of their womb, priests flowing blood
onto the leaves of lives
filed in draft board drawers
students staining fountains carmine,
trudging placards over asphalt
day after month after year.
Many wrote then strident poems
bitter poems too near events for hope.
Too near events our decade
tore our marriage apart
though both of us lived it honestly,
though each of us ended up with
distinctions we mightn't have chosen.

Preludium

Under sloping skylights
cattleyas and wax flowers
cascade from my desk loft
that overlooks our dining room.
Seen from below, their beady
glass magenta hearts *Hoya carnosa*
glisten in re-curved petals
thick as candle drippings.
Warm days like this
they drop to the hardwood floor
with irregular soft thuds that
                make us laugh.
My eighth-grade daughter and I
are reading mail and doing homework.
These easy times I love to recall
her pointing to some crows and saying,
"Look, Mommy, those birds are waving to me."

We jump with delight to read
she can go to Cal
for summer pre-calculus
to begin a path
we hope will be clearer than mine.
That very day we register
celebrate with a Coke at student union.
Perched on the balcony's edge
a sleek flute player
airs us Bach's *Preludium*
the chortling repetitions
I've just been teaching her
on our new black shiny piano.
We take it for a sign that she belongs here.
Then she says she saw him pass
                and he waved
the boy I'd pointed out at church.

Confirmation class appealed
until the priest assigned too much
and she turned to quadratic equations instead.

Dark humid August afternoon
distant thunder, heavy droplets
          merely remind us
of the relief that rain could bring.
She sits on the floor in her room
          delightedly composing
captions for full page photographs
wide-eyed furry creatures
from Ranger Rick nature magazine.
She places them with tape
to hang on her walls between
massive writhing handsome rock stars
stretching slippery sweat-spangled bodies
heatedly around electric guitars.
*"Mom, I'm never gonna marry anyone
        whose parents aren't divorced!"*

Evening settles on Albany valley's
carapace of roofs and trees,
evenly spotted with soft street lights.
The cleansing smell as fog slides in
veiling the town lavender,
under indigo sky and early stars.
Droning foghorns underscore
raptor cries over Albany Hill.

A few years later hot refusal
to attend Catholic school
two of them scolded for four-inch heels
black jumpsuits, eyeliner,
defiance-wrested control.
Dark and not home yet,
she's claimed her life, and I will read
late into night, listening.

The shared calls of night hawks
fuse the valley below our hillside house.

High on another hill, an earlier house
Santa Claus brought gymnastics class
to dispel a year that memory constricts,
sports car speeding down strange roads
both of us crying out for each other.
"Some things shouldn't be happened."
In that house I cried a lot,
she learned to safely answer the door by herself.
New, the two of us, against old ways.

At last well employed, dignity
beyond what anyone I knew
would have hoped for any woman.
And still my family said I should give her up
to a stranger, yet another new wife
        with far more money
        to give her more
when only eight percent of U.S. women's
        incomes were exceeding mine,
        my office was in our home,
        and she could travel with me if I wanted.
Terrible years we made it through,
"Something is wrong with something, isn't it Mommy?"

A few years before, we'd slept on the floor
in front of the fire on silky quilts
so my bedroom could be a room
filled with toys for children
        who stayed all day
that I might go to school at night.
Loving those children and watching my daughter play
gave spirit to break the bounds of woman's world.
By music reborn and courage imagined
the world believed us,

though many times I had to tell her
we were just as good as families
who still had fathers and more kids.
Finally her fifth grade principal told me
    fifty-five percent of schoolmates
        came from single parent households.
And for the first time I felt that we were normal.

William, Cat Burial Poem

All day I've noticed spaces usually occupied
by you, this morning expected your feet to twitch
as usual, lying on my sunny bedspread
or your head to lift quickly as I set down a glass
on the tabletop, your eyes to open.

While my daughter gathers roses
from our twenty-seven bushes
I hold you like a baby thanking you
for giving back into our days
the loving and the playing
poured out from my child to you.

You look like a Hawaiian celebration
how we've covered you with flowers.
She's carefully with concentration
placed each rose in just the right position
according to her sense of you.
Sweet Williams, pink and purple daisies
we fitted into the blanket of roses,
scented geraniums under your face
and red coral bells over all.
Our favorite plants express how much we loved you,
keep us from seeing
the soil that sifts through our fingers
    touch your fur.
Powdered earth between the petals
dazes us as slowly, handful by heavy handful
    you disappear.
Soon an umber blanket is punctuated
with shards of vibrant color.

My daughter sobs, my voice breaks as I tell her
things she needs to know
about dying and loving, living and gathering soul,

my arms around her, face against my chest.
"I don't want him to be dead,
*   I don't want him to be dead."*

As we're spreading fragrant leaves
on top of the grave she says,
"Only the new ones, the red ones, only new growth."
She sits and hugs me, crying.
Finally I kiss her cheek and forehead
and say to go lie down on my bed.
She picks up our temperamental ten-year-old tabby
who's been watching it all from several feet away.
She folds her in her arms
on the flowered quilt
and she scratches the kitty's back
and murmurs to her for awhile
and her desperate sorrow begins to relax and subside.

Forty

Me, I do waste my time.
        I sit for a long time
                I look around
I wander and chat
            I watch other people
and I'm beginning to prefer to think
        that I'm more like other people
                than not.
I am just living this life
        not really making
                too much of it
                      right now
not achieving
        what I'd have thought
                I would, by now.
I've sat in alot of sun, felt
            breezes, heard birds, kids, cars
                    gotten sad, angry, glad.
I see the orange plastic sign
            on the franchise restaurant
                          and don't hate it anymore.

Burney Creek

Here in a ringing fugue the river falls
    splashes past grassy isles,
        billowing hillocks that stand
    like jades in close museum lights.
Ballooning crests overhang to the water's surface,
      their tall gold stands bear still spring's dried rosettes,
        now autumn's airy diadems.
Undulant islands of lace–
    white cupped flowers
        on stiff little shaking stems
        embroidered over the stream,
    pearls to ransom an imprisoned heart.

Light breaks dusted through the trees
    emblazons tapestries that pulse
      like rustling taffeta, incessant choir
        of the poet's shook foil.
Winding downriver
    the graced parabolas of my cast fly line
      sweep across curling eddies. They dip and surge
loosen, expand, and open again
    roll along to the next constellations of rock.
Like Venetian paperweights
    under viscous glassy water
      lie boulders fleeced with cress plants,
        brilliant domes verdant as malachite
          luscious as emeralds.

Thighs pressed against the current
I fumble for steps between stones furred with moss.
    The river pulls my footholds
and balancing forward I catch
    moist fragrances of humus, and hear
    rolling boulders' underwater booms,
signaling resettling.

        Joy breaks deep in the dark of my bones
        where words need not translate the wisdom we hear.
And dun-colored shorebirds and sleek dragonflies
        speed across the stream's enameled surface,
            cry out high-pitched certainties.
Crystal rapids shatter forth the songs
     of the year's visitations,
          reminiscing before the freeze.

Owl

Last year an owl perched on my casement window
        lowered his head under the frame
to level metallic yellow eyes at mine.
For awhile I was part of his rounds.
He would land on the edge of the roof and screech
        till I set aside my books, leaned out
              and acknowledged him eye to eye.
His claws would scratch on the tiles a bit longer
        and then he would fly on into the night.
I was proud that he came by.

Swallows now twitter and swoop
        about the house at early evening
              picking up bits of dirt for mud nests.
Yesterday I watched while two of them
        circled and dived at one another
            touching beaks
        and flirted about on the balcony railing,
as though in their travels they'd seen
        the shape of time hugging
              the ceaseless round of the ocean's edge,
as though they'd found time only goes in circles
        and only to give them back to each other.

At daybreak a fiery press of twinking gold
        lines the lower edge of my skylight,
its condensed droplets of sun
        blind me to the remembered blue above
        conceal what they soon might be.
For several months now I've been
        wondering over some question,
            still I do not know.
But I have noticed that one set of events
        becomes settled in some aspects

   and surges in others,
  inclines toward unexpected dimensions,
then without a noticeable moment
   arches into the next set of occurrences.

Pink Moon Descending

This dark at last has lost the struggle
        to the buoy's throaty rings.
      A squeaky shorebird's
tinny scratching at the surface of the day,
        steadily rising freeway sounds
behind my Emeryville waterfront condo.
Address books kept in pencil, goals unstated
        prized books unread.
At my desk till midnight nights on end
        for the money,
and even managing new investments
        I do a lot of staring out the window.
        I don't even bother recording
anecdotes confided by acclaimed
        acquaintances, or getting autographs.
Even now waiting,
        waiting to make something better.

Pink moon descending
        over Golden Gate headlands
SF windows flash white lights
        back at the sunrise behind us.
The bridge of course glows postcard orange
        and nephrite Tamalpias slopes into
            a dark blue topaz bay.
I watch from my bed
        the light move higher
        the light move higher and out into the world
and I daily pray for stamina to follow.

I-80

California

Donner Pass storm
ice on asphalt, beat of chains
sliding cars, snow banks.
Pulling their car behind a rented truck
holding her newborn son.
So long to sit
so soon after caesarean.
Over and over in my mind
her voice, over again her reasons
for leaving the West.
"If you think you need to move back there, we can do that."
Familiar ring, I've known that love.
Apache marriage prayer
For you both, the days
of loneliness are through, for you
there will be no more loneliness.
In my daughter's life there is no loneliness.
Blessed is the fruit.

Remembering when first I was with her,
lavender tablecloth
carried through a eucalyptus valley
behind the Berkeley hills
to find a hidden grove of Monterey pines
to relish this secret that so far only I knew
this child at last in my body.
Sipping lapsang souchong tea
falling asleep on smoky sun warmed needles.

Passing the land of gold
land of her ancestors
her great, great-grandmother
born nearby, married in Sweetland
kept rooms and cooked for boarders,

kitchen table surgery
blessed among women.
The rest of his life her
nearly blind school teacher husband
often sat, quietly holding
her braid, her long dark
auburn hair across his knees
stroking her hair, remembering.

            Nevada
No call means they made it across the pass.
Sparks, Fernley, the great desert.
Scratched-in roads to active mines by day
by night the winking towers of power plants.
Lovelock, letters painted high on hillsides
Winnemucca, Battle Mountain
Carlin, Elko, Wells.
Land of ranchers, sheep and cattle,
rustlers, trucker with double rig that
edged our car with California plates
onto a narrow shoulder at Battle Mountain
where cavalry wars left multitudes of arrow heads.
Mother Mary. Pray for us.
Range after desert mountain range
formed from lava bulging through stretched earth.

            Hawai'i
Under a Kona coffee orchard's
heavy scarlet jade vine,
chatting of my daughter's years at Cal
her studying with friends
in Bancroft coffee houses.
Lattes, many lattes.
Queen Ka'ahumanu's necklace, hundreds of tiny braids
hair of friends gathered to hold
the carved bone tongue, symbol of royalty.

Feed my four dozen year-old trees
raised from gathered coffee cherries
replant orchids in hāpu'u under the jacarandas
pick up yellow passion fruits
prizes half hidden in leaves.
Start Hawaiian purple potato bread
set out long rice to soak
rest my hand on the glass stemmed turquoise soap dish,
a middle school Mothers Day gift,
and the molded glass butter dish cover
her first garage sale discovery.

Utah

The Great Salt Lake
figuring probable distances
to keep track where she is
by now past roads
I know so well to Idaho,
I have to look to roadmaps
in order not to lose her.
Once, I let
her out of sight.
In Honolulu.
Overprotective, friends said.
She could walk
half a block to buy
the little toy.
Together downstairs to the street,
return to second floor to watch
but she must have
got there before I
got back here.
Watch five minutes for her to leave the store
go back to greet her on the street.
Watch as I walk
expect to see her emerge from the store's
front door. CLOSED. Ran and

Searched and Asked and
Called the whole two blocks to Kalākaua
heard her voice across
the four lane, peopled, busy boulevard
"Mommy," smiling, waving, *"I'm over here,"*
already the stranger's candy in her hand.
I shiver as I write.
Now and at the hour of our death.

                    Wyoming
The Overlanders' Route
buffalo lands, blizzards. By night
the map-colored shapes of
states she's crossing
string across my darkness.
Portrait of pioneer woman holding infant,
the mother's eyes that look past mine
into the place where she will have known
the cost of moving forward.
Rock Springs, Laramie, Cheyenne
onto the plains, crossing
lands of Geronimo
Chief Joseph, Sitting Bull.
Forty thousand people
pre-contact.
Same as Hawai'i
where Queen Lili'u's favorite plant
crownflower
white as the sugar
that stole her reign,
draws returning monarchs to my yard
for months each spring.

No blizzard forecast. In mind's dark
I see their caravan
cross bleak stretches
her dogs curled at her feet
her son beside her on the wide truck seat,

and I ache at the curve of the earth that arcs between us.
Mother Mary, in my daughter's life.

Hawai'i
Return of beloved spirits
Dia de los Muertos
albondigas soup
meatballs dropped in disappear
then rise one by one.
Remembering she'd come home from grade school
proudly make herself a quesadilla.
Now Halloween visits
from three best cowgirl friends
small hands full of chocolate candies.
There is no loneliness.
Evening stitching
my Baltimore Album quilt
patterns from cheery Aunt Lilly.

Nebraska
Cather country, amber waves
first to grant women equal rights.
Lincoln, Ogallala, North Platte
miles wide river, inches deep.
Here our ancestor started his wagon train
with tools, wheat, corn from outfitters.
Buffalo grasslands
cut across
by railroads to the future.
Omaha, Council Bluffs, Iowa
bandstands, cakewalks, state fair country,
marching bands.

Iowa
Riverboats. Rolling farmlands saved
from bankruptcy by corn-fat pigs.
Land of trading posts, forts, and quilts.

Our first time apart was her father's
annual summer visit to Iowa.
To endure her absence I used
all my earnings to explore
Hawai'i, land of my dreams.
Now in Ft. Dodge she can place her son
in his great-grandmother's arms.
She was three years old
when I had to tell her not to be afraid
when I cried from stress and fear in divorce.
"It's all right, Mommy, I know you love me."
In elementary school she asked
what religion was, I said it was
living our life according to the highest love we know.
Then she said, *"We're Hawaiian, aren't we, Mommy."*

Remembering schoolmate Jenny
with us on her first trip outside
California. Hiked to Jenny Lake
their laughing, managing together
to fall in the creek, to hike back wet to the car
inventing verses to Carmen's aria
all about our lost keys.
But at fifteen her glaring eyes
struck fear into my heart
when I'd insisted she return early
from her boyfriend's midweek
band practice.
Remembering my nightmares
when first she moved under
a different roof than mine.
Proud in her first apartment
houseplants all over
flowered plates we'd used when she was little
furniture I'd saved for her
linens, rugs, my red enamel pots and pans
tulip mugs she'd always liked.
But for me it was Time's jag-toothed saw

drawing near, skin torn
from my chest, no other
way for dreams to say it
images, dreams' only words.

Later her ardent interest in white sharks
planning three months on the Farallones.
Places in her life I must not reach.
Finally, dives to research gobies,
pareu lifestyle
night swims with friends across
tropical island channels.

Hawai'i

Sort negatives and photos
return calls, cull books
from overflowing shelves.
Hem a satin robe to send
for mid-night nursings in wintry Michigan.
Check long distance rates to Detroit.
Stitching, stitching.
Hike Hualāla'i with Bill.

Hula rehearsal at Hulihe'e Palace
waves crash, spray cools
the mothervoice sings, my feet caress the grass
the rhythm's sway   steadying   as gravity
draws my body   back   into my soul.
The mothervoice sings
of our similar   sea turtle dreams,
swimming slowly   dream-eyed
ribbons of kelp   grow on her shell
sheltering clusters   of clinging shrimps
snails, limpets   little fishes that
make their homes   within.
And the princess of the sea   *(pause)*
who woke my daughter   just in time.
Wearing the green jade   pendant she gave me

seashell necklace she made of yarn,
and green glass leaf shaped earrings.
The strands of their hair placed around her neck.

Treading Pu'u O'o
at Kamoamoa

Molten field of bulged upwellings
      spreads new flows in broad black fans
      heaves against brittle crusting folds
grainy flaming edges crushing over
      spiky crags of jagged rock
          the *a'ā*
              formed by being broken.

Rivers of metals rumble underfoot
      through benches and shelves of new-hardened lava
air shimmers above earth's birthing fever,
and heat-glazed, expectant
      I hurry toward the outflow.
High pitched snaps of cracking glass
      close-by explosions of methane
          smoldering dragon's breath and gusting winds.
Pele's core pours fluorescent
      into crashing surf,
ocean hisses her retaliation
      spits strong stinky
          sulfurous blasts
      furious sand filled fulminations of steam.
Hieratic battle of the goddesses.
Open crevices. *Mysterium Tremendum.*

          2.

I climb down new-cooled bluffs to gather
      sand fresh formed, washed in from waves
and recall my daughter, nearly seven
      playing all day on Hilo Bay's black shore
with rocks and shells, whatever's given
      with drifted wood and floating plastic,
her repeated attempts to believe
      that the ocean would hold her up.
      In rubber sandals and homemade mu'umu'u

we walked toward Halema'uma'u crater
        flaking lava crunching underfoot.
Cracks in the firepit's surface separated
        to reveal the tangerine pool
brought forth from the belly of the earth.
        Iron of our blood.
        Strength of our bones.

        3.

My mind begins prayers now
    for protection
    memories, losses integrated
    gratitude for what was good.
I stare into grasstops blowing unburned
and remember being speechless at her birth.
Then attempts to layer over
        petrify maternal instincts
            submerged in service of separation
under a different roof than mine.
Women in India, getting ready,
      might give away a favorite jewel
        on a daughter's birthday.
Earth tears open pouring forth new land.
The great woman, broadly spreading Mauna Loa
      the sinewy braids of her shiny black twisting hair
        the long rolling pleats of her skirts.
Paved in successive layers of hardened lava
    she spills forth from within
        again and again
            expansive generation.

We grasp the sand to ask the earth to hold us
    add our offering, sand or shell or poem
to ti, anthuriums, crown flower lei
    bits of jewelry, piles of rocks.
Wordless, Pele speaks across the decades,
    and we too relinquish *heiau*, past desires
        accept her flowing reconstructions.

Pu'u Loa Petroglyphs

Open ocean outrigger canoes
    crossed opposing currents
    at South Point
to bring for consecrated burial
    umbilical cords.
Returning to Pele a part of her own.
Under clouds of volcanic steam
    supplicants made offerings
    the hair of a king, ōhelo berries.
They blessed the goddess's bounties
    chanted the volcano's awesome hunger
    to swallow a village
    to take back fish ponds
        kings had built.
They begged its abstinence from the rest.
Returning to her lava body again.

Stacked stone *ahu*
    offer prayers for the unconceived
    plead for safe birth.
How many of us
    or our babies
    or our birthing daughters
would have survived?
Burials framed with carved-in rings
    simple one-inch holes covered with stones
    some in clusters
    others linear.
A figure etched with five umbilical circles
    placed between extended thighs.
Another depicting legs widespread
    in open birth position
    two small human figures in between.
Buried in undulant ropes of her hair.

Shining *pāhoehoe* river, sea of light
black earth rounded, bulbous with belly fat
      as Mesopotamia's Venus of Willendorf
female folds and crevices
      soft as many breasted Artemis of Ephesus.
Cracks in wavy surfaces cubed apart
      reveal spongy, placental underlayers
      a once emerging bulb within a vent.
Pathways of granular, crunchy lava
      sands flaked off by sudden cooling.
Her ropy hair covers her body in curves.

On this mountain's sides I sang to my child
      of stars exploding above and fires below,
      passion for the earth's fantastic life.
Here I've scribed my soul's story
      like ancients
      who scratched their meanings
      into the ropy waves of Pele's hair.
Here on this land most recently
      born from Pele's fiery womb
we come to touch the source
      nearest the goddess's
      own bringing forth.
Returning to Pele a part of her own.
Mother of Land, Mother of Blood
Mother of Wonder, Mother of Spirit.
Ropes of her long black hair cover the curves of her body.

Call Notes From Hakalau

From too many years of biting her tongue
    my daughter's unsaid words hold their fire
        burning white sores into her mouth.
A hundred ōhi'a trees have heard her name
    as we are re-foresting high in Hakalau.
Ancient koa raise pleading limbs
while amakihi whistles and trills
    punctuate the throaty wood bell song
        of apapane clucks and calls
that wraps all landscape forms together,
    weds clouds to leaves to soil
        weaves trunks and tree ferns into one another
in the unexpected opaline glow
        of upland midday shade.
Cushioned in grasses my listening body
    aches to restore her laughter
        the humor, devotion she's known for.
Like slightly shifting kaleidoscope bits
    some birdsong strength
        has got to cast new light,
re-constellate the balances of her life.
A hundred ōhi'a trees have heard her name.

Positions

His elbow in my rib cage
        my grandson's head
                fragile shoulders
                      lie on my belly.
Every half hour he flops
        pushing different ways
against my chest, thighs.
        Arms around me
                sighs, little snores
                      sleep talking.
He lifts his velour pillow
        taps the bed beneath it
"Put your arm right there,"
        returns at once to dreams.
Can lack of sleep
        coverless cold, predawn hunger
                even longevity really matter
as much as this soft head
        cupped in my hand.

Language Arts

"Grandma, why is there
    Language Arts when there
        isn't any art in language?"
After popcorn, kids building with Legos
    in front of the fireplace,
        me ear plugged.
Two boys insisting at one another
    sudden rule-switching invented as they go
spurred by tiny testosterone surges
    propulsive words rough on the roof of the mouth
        sizzling past lips, practicing.

At least till the bedtime snuggle and singing begins.
Then the mind pulls in around itself
    resigns itself to culture,
always Merwin's *Sorrow String*
    slipping in its note,
"Grandma, we always miss Mommy, don't we?"
If you want to watch desire structure your day
    push a five-year-old in a shopping cart
        through Target or Longs.
His primordial bond with stuff's in constant motion.

Language Arts II

Sean at seven proving in the mind that there is
No such thing as nothing.
If someone says there is
No such thing as nothing
And looks at the air in front of him
He has to say
"I don't see anything. I see nothing."
That is the same thing as saying that
"Nothing is there." So nothing is really something.

So there is
No such thing as there being nothing.
Or rather, I can't see anything
But I know the air is there
So it is not nothing
Even though I see nothing.
So there is no such thing as nothing.

Puzzle For Sean, age 10

It is said that:

Absence Makes The Heart Grow Fonder

And also that:

All That Glitters Is Not Gold

We know from Science that:

Absence (though fonder) Is Assuredly Yonder

And we know from Feeling that:

[Absence...] [...Is Not Golden]

Thus by Subtraction we delete:

[Absence...]

And:

[...Is Not Gold]

Therefore the Equation tells us:

All That Glitters Makes The Heart Grow Fonder.

Aquinas' Logic

We see that all things pass in and out of existence.
If it is possible for every thing not to exist
Then at some time nothing did exist.
So Something began causing existence.

MH's Logic

We see that all physical life is subject to decomposition.
Decomposed objects are eventually re-incorporated
into physical entities.
Then nothing falls out of existence, but its elements
are re-arranged.
So nothing passes out of existence.
Bill said Einstein thought of this before MH did.

Genuine divination,
in short, has
nothing whatsoever
to do with
natural law…
It is not concerned
at all
with
the way in which
a phenomenon–
be it event,
person,
or thing–
came into
existence,
but with
what it means,
that is,
with its
significance as a 'sign'
of the holy.

DC Poem

Sean distracts his mother in our descent
        stroking her arm, *"It will be all right"*
        but she cries anyway, every landing.
"The Potomac!" And, *"Look, a lighthouse."*
Heavy rain threads zip across the wing
        a steeple in mist, buildings, *"Is that Watergate?"*
Seat backs up, carried-on stuff back under the seat ahead,
'We're here' calls to home
        three generations of fingers entwined in relief.
The pilot comes on, "Ladies and Gentlemen,
        here in DC we've got a mess On The Ground."
Reagan 'Mr. Airline De-regulation' Airport.
One of 2008's biggest words,
        now that three decades of it have brought us
            the sound a grassfire makes in grain.

But, 'On The Ground' and 'Going Forward'–
        every decade has its terms–
the first hallway poster we see
        is the local power company
flashing Obama's "Yes We Can" portrait
        under their slogan:
"We bring electricity to the country."

Our luxuriously affordable seedy hotel
        those one-inch hexagonal tiles
            in black and white
                on the bathroom floor,
        not even worth bringing the electrical
            up to code,
no possibility of pretension here.
        Comfortable enough, always friendly.
An April evening walk to the National Mall
        every direction locates the Washington Monument,
            obelisks and such as sign of the father

           though he insisted he must not
                    be thought of as monarch,
          towering icon of purity
          but blood-stain red in setting sun
                    from the Vietnam Memorial.
                    Far far far too many names to count.

The Capitol dome in a storm cloud sky
          behind a spread of level dogwood blossoms,
their flat but softly curving oval petals
          bunched at the center
                    with two dozen chartreuse oblong capsules,
creases running the length of the petals,
          a bruised spillway pinched out from each tip.

Morning walk past turquoised statues
          heroes tall in early damp air
and the iron-fenced White House garden's
          softening fragrance from some
                    unseen blossom,
          and soothing robin calls.
Inscribed stone paths approach the fountains
          at the World War II Memorial
          where Erica crouches for photos in chill light.
The glistening curve of a gold-mounted wall,
                    its gleaming fabric of gold-plate stars
casts the wide gold of all the stars' faces
          onto the water, dark below.
A man sweeping tells us every star
          stands for one hundred deaths.
                    Far far far too many stars to count.
Sean reads, *"Here we mark the price of freedom."*

Presidents' words cut in stone
          "...to oppose tyrannical oppression..."
                    this year echo reversals in my mind.
We circle the pond, ringed with each battle's name
          European fronts on the south

                    Pacific on the north
and I break into sudden sobbing
          trying to photograph my father's great-grandson,
                    his look-alike, in front of Guadalcanal.
Later Sean stands
          on the elevated landing
                    before the main fountain
                              willing to be photographed
               in shoulders-back posture, his chin up
          serious eyes gaze straight into mine
compassionate, as though he's heard some word from afar.

Behind him at each of four compass points
a four-arched pavilion shelters
          four mighty brown-bronze eagles,
                    their upward reaching, undulant wings'
                         spread tip-feathers barely touch.
                         Beak-held
                    ribbon garlands
               counter wing angles,
          hold level a wreath
of overlapping leaves.
Steely claws clasp dome-topped pillars.
Balance of Fours, symmetry, stability.
               Quaternity.

Lush low walkway wall of espaliered wisteria
          pillowy layers of lavender in long chains,
                    like soft silk tassels inviting touch.
My father's pride in his purple wisteria
          cascading four stories up to our roof,
that voluminous fragrance of citrus flowers
          both creamy and sharp at the same time.

Then breakfast at the Museum Of The American Indian
          after my Bent Grandmother Dance
          to recorded drum chants at the door.
So many tribes and languages,

their lighted names filled the continent
        with the long proof.
Wilted from roaming the landscapes of sorrow
        inhabited by my three generations before me,
            my great-grandfather a wagon train leader–
        they named their town Brown's Valley for him–
I slump deep into a leather chair
        to await my next two generations.

In matched plaid skirts
        navy vests, ribboned pony tails
            three 11-year-olds
gaze into interactive screens
        each pressing prompts
        to change the image
busily showing each other what can be done.
        And to an adult,
        "Mom! You can open drawers,
        they really are drawers."
And never-not-once looked up at the lighted cases
        two feet in front of them
            displaying baskets and intricate beading.

First priority: Natural History's
Early Life and Stromatolites.
Soon after earth condensed
        from spinning, dusty clouds
        four billion years ago,
was it so easy for life itself to arise
        from simple chemicals that began to form long chains?
Simple chemicals react in simple conditions
        in light and heat, building complexity,
long chains that wrapped themselves into miniscule life
        that reproduced, building complexity,
            and reproduced. Variety….variety.
These tiny heroes, cyano-bacteria
        used the sun to transform earth
            two billion years ago.

They cut in on the ever changing
      dance of the hydrogen bond
      that switches partners billions of times a second.
Cutting in to spin off oxygen,
        cyano-bacteria secreted a gluey substance
that collected sand in wavy tight crusted layers,
      built domed mounds rising from tides
releasing O_2 from seawater. Enough O_2
      eventually forming Atmosphere
      eventually formed the Ozone Layer
      that sheltered Life.

Second Day: Erica's out to catch dawn light
      on the Vietnam wall.
Under a tree for a ten minute downpour
       a vet told her stories about a few names on the wall
         his high school classmate,
           one bachelor who'd pulled three dads to safety,
         another guy whose friend had died in his arms.
Back in our room for coffee and chocolate,
     "So, I'll have 2 hours to meet you guys for lunch
     and then after 3 I'm free again."
Her National Conference of Teachers of Mathematics,
      all her department's money to her for this meeting
        for her expertise at raising kids to grade level.
But not like De-regulation math:

<u>(Pre-)Algebra</u> (7th graders only)
Hmm. Let's see. If you have
Valued a bond assuming 10%
Is the X number of sub-prime
Contents, What Would its Value be
If X is *really* 95% ??

Sean and Grandma walking to the Mall
see a patrol car blocking Pennsylvania Ave,
we pause to consider turning back
then instantly know to

"Hurry, Going Forward!"
And we barely get there,
"Sean, that's the President's car!"
And he's in it
    heading I'm guessing to address
        Congressional leaders
on Treasury moves for economic rescue
    for damage from America's shadow banks.
The line of official vehicles stretched to a dozen
    swollen after the sixties to include
    at least four emergency medical trucks
    and two assault vans camo-ed as SUVs.
A passerby asks, "What was that?"
"The President's motorcade."
"Really? Really?!! Wow!!"
Counting our strides going home we measure
84 steps we'd stood from Obama,
like everyone here in DC
    measuring our position
    in relation to centers of power.

From The Ground Up, rising through twisted strappy leaves
    yolk-bright yellow tulips foreground
        the Capitol dome, now framed in steely clouds
            opening into narrow strips of blue.

The Hall of Minerals' astonishing crystal specimens
    and rough rocks beside their stunning gem cuts,
    jewels from coarse, how would they feel to hold?
The famed Hope Diamond, set in a gap-toothed circlet
    of enough weighty solitaires
        for sixteen Wall Street wives or mistresses
            to display the jewels that prove
        he's mightier than others, that prove
        he's garnered most
            of everyone's pie for himself,
    that possibly death won't strip him of his story.

Solitaires gap-toothed and gaudy beside
the American-flag-blue unlikelihood
    of forty-five carats of crystal clarity,
that negligee satin twilight blue
    that creases into azure highlights,
that sudden deep water blue
    as you swim off the edge of the reef,
      still flashing its turquoise highlights
        into the depths,
and those silver white gleams shining off the surface.

At the Korean Memorial the three of us parka-ed
    mirrored in walls, our many hands
      touching their faces
our pensive reflections place us in front lines,
    etched soldiers in battle gear
      advancing from the reflected trees behind us,
        today's blue sky showing through.
And in the wall we see them
    backing us up from farther behind,
the life size bronze soldiers
    in combat helmets, boot length rain capes
      two-way radios' long antennae.

Black tiled shallow pool filled with pennies,
    rippling sky, tree trunks
and inscribed:
Dead   USA 54,246   UN   628,833
Missing   USA 8,177   UN   470,267

Erica joins us a part of each day.
Them avoiding mud, walking the edge
of the Lincoln Memorial's long reflecting pool
    the distant temple's fluted Doric pillars
      reaching all the way down the water to us.
Them sitting on a wall
    framed in a flag blue sky
the Lincoln's carved eagle cornice barely showing behind.

Erica photos me lying flat
>   the stone bench's cold
>   pressed into my back.
Them going into the Lincoln
>   then coming back to say
>   that I must climb the stairs and stand before him.
"It is for us the living, rather, to be dedicated here
>   *to the unfinished work*
>   *which they who fought here*
>   *have thus far so nobly advanced."*

Every evening crossing the Mall's big playfield
>   filled with soccer games and Frisbees,
every evening strolling back to town
>   for Corona with aspirin and laughter
>   dinners always the same Italian restaurant.
Healing my back, and hearing them sleep
>   the city center quiet enough
>   for air from open windows.
Morning chat and room-made coffee
>   p-b and j, sharing tight space.
Crutches left in the closet after day one
>   walk two miles each day and four on the fifth
>   on prednisone's false mobility.
The three of us:
>   *"You two are talking about me"*
>   *"Where did it go?!" "Where did she go?"*
>   *"Where could she be?"*
>   *"I'm not a total idiot" "I need a new memory card"*
>   *"Teacher's ears"*
>   *"Strike iron while it is hot"*
>   *"If we're lucky enough to be in DC together,*
>   *we're lucky enough."*
Five April days that moved from winter to summer
>   the last day's evening picnic on the grass.
What was it that was like
>   the lacework of light
>   from reflections off ripples

    under the arches of a low bridge,
    the low bridge over the Potomac?

So often back to Natural History:
    This was my favorite place
       even over all the art museums.
    This is where I kept
thinking of bringing grandchildren
         when first I saw it all with Bill.
Fossils of a dinosaur that took to air
    how the moon and seas were formed
      the mountains and volcanoes.
Large fossils shaped in active poses
      on murals of their filled out selves,
claw-spread regal leaping tigers, standing Kodiaks
     a basement full of butterflies.
Creatures, so many enchanting creatures,
    some theologians say that creatures
       are God's words.

Most days indeed the new life swarms
    as groups of junior high schoolers mob the halls
     hordes of them mocking and pulling at each other.
Who can blame their restlessness?
Yawnful hours in lines
    the ante-room filled to capacity
     with locate-me-colored matching T-shirts
for the RunAroundTourOfTheCongress' underground tunnels.
A chamber in session is nearly empty
    seven members taking their turns at the lectern
    to shake their fists and yell into TV cameras
"And I told them, told them all…"
    explaining to Sean that they want their voters
      to see them taking their tabloid stands
        on everything, anything, anything at all.
What was it the founders envisioned would happen here?
    In fact, *"Just what is the evil*
      that we must fight or else be overcome by?"

We missed the Woolworth luncheon counter
      where the first sit-in took place,
but saw the Supreme Court's nine chairs empty
        the old dark comfort of chocolate brown leather
          and long-polished walnut,
    where soon they would block the ban
        on corporate political spending.
"Democracy is now the trophy wife of free-market capitalism."
                            -MHL, <u>DC Poem</u>
"The test of our progress is not whether we add more to the abundance of those who have much; it is whether we provide enough to those who have too little."
                              -FDR (and Eleanor's
bronze-green fingers bright with the peoples' caresses.)

"Ask not what America will do for you but what together we can do for the freedom of man."   -JFK

National Geographic engineer,
Kyler– dive buddy of Erica's at Cal–
explains to Sean, twelve, seated in a swivel chair
the animal-mounted camera project
      how his team's working on problems
           of film losing color at certain depths.
Sean makes a suggestion
      K gave E a look of surprise and said,
"Well, we're exploring just that idea right now."
Then seeing the split screen
      run footage and data together,
"Can you hook it up to location
      to tell where the whale and data were recorded?"
"We're trying to figure out how to do that.
      We can only see what the animal's looking at."
"Can you mount one on the back?"
      "We've usually got a size issue with that."
Discussion of camera size ensued.
Hypotheses and Exchanges.

"First time I've ever talked
    with an engineer about his job."
Proudly acclaimed by Sean
    as his only adult interaction.

Riding the Metro to Arlington Cemetery
    to see the Kennedy graves, their words,
JFK: *"Here on earth God's work must surely be our own."*
And Bobby said, *"Some men see things, and say Why?*
    I dream things that never were, and ask Why not?"

And the cherry blossoms…
    only a decades old weeping cherry
can hide its black-brown structure
    in clusters of balls
        of clusters of petals,
can induce a thick pink oblivion
    to the very same colors
        in Jackie's suit that day.

Then Sean wanting to solve the Metro system,
he could At The End Of The Day maneuver us
from Metro Center to Gallery Place on Red
    to L'Enfant Plaza on Green
        to Federal Center on Blue
on our way to meet Mom
    at the Museum Of The American Indian for dinner.
And halfway there when two ladies asked me directions
    he said, *"Yes, you're on the right level,*
yours will be the next train in four minutes
    and you'll get off at the second stop."

Sean's patient attention a requisite hour
    to the world's finest painters
his candid curiosity
    at Leonardo's brushless details,
his delight and laughter in the mysteries
    of modern sculpture's myriad puzzles.

A standing figure made from springs
        and curling strips of rusted metal.
A mobile's arching steel arms
          hung with black ovals, perfectly balanced
              to move with slight air currents.
The endless connected loops of cast iron ribbon
        placed on a pedestal at the entrance.
Sean beams crouched under the bulky, scrotal belly
      of the nine-foot welded spider,
             its peak jointed muscular legs.

Always back and forth on the Mall
from Magna Carta
    to Declaration
        and Constitution
from museums to monuments and fountains.

The fourth afternoon too tired to stand any longer
we hit the 3D at Natural History:
"Eight nights after
    the August full moon
the feather starfish gather,
    releasing ova and sperm
in a voluminous cloud..."
        that must reflect some lacework of light within them.

Our last hours at the Air and Space Museum:
        where we touched a rock that was brought
            from the moon
    walked through the Skylab
    looked into tiny Apollo spacecrafts
        the Apollo II space module
          complete with see thru cabinet
              labeled "Life Vests."
    Saw again the film
        of the actual first moon landing
a satellite, space photos of earth
a Russian missile from the Cuban crisis

      the Wright brothers' paired moth-white wings
          their trailing edges twisted
              and slightly drooping toward each other.
  These two who were sure they could figure it out,
      what started it all in motion above the earth.

Even against the greatest odds
    there is something in the human spirit–
        a magic blend of skill, faith, and valor–
that can lift men from certain defeat
    to incredible victory.   -FDR

With the progress of the human mind
    as new discoveries are made
    new truths discovered
      and manners and opinions change,
With the change of circumstances
    institutions must advance also
    to keep pace with the times.
We might as well require a man
    to wear still the coat
    which fitted him when a boy
As civilized society to remain ever under
    the regimen of their barbarous ancestors.
                -Thomas Jefferson

Part IV

Mirror Ulua

Mirror Ulua

Dreams' depths harbor
        glinting silver dollar fishes
whose fin-thread banners–
        silver, turquoise, black,
like sunbeams that slant
        through mind's shallow surf–
draw parallels, point
        to symbols written
            in the sands of my flesh.

And…ah!
        when they recoil
            and several turn as one,
a surreptitious apparition
        tells nature's true intent:
ribbon dancers
        poets of the sea
flourish the waters
        of sleep's alchemy
script curves of disguise
        encircle the real with semblances
            of stinging tentacles.

The scansion of their hesitant
        acceding bridal pace
casts unmasking veils
        of oblique words,
            words that silence or repeat
                interfere, delay
as to oppose or evoke. Perhaps they
        bridge a gap, cut across
some lack, aligning me again
        in the gaze of some archaic other.

As butterflies that look like leaves

        these ambiguous arabesques
              surprise me into open-mindedness.
This mimicry
      this heart of metaphor
swims through my solitude
        complicating preconceptions,
gently uncovers
          lodestone constellations–
              humbling vulnerabilities,
      those wilder beauties of my truth.

                    for Ron Spinka

Gold and Angelfood
> *We find in the scansion of our hesitations*
> *the ordering of the unconscious*
> *to the desire of the Other.* Jacques Lacan

Sleek as an art nouveau dragonfly
    detailed in fine black lines
the pale yellow Spark stove,
    trimmed in that Coke bottle dull green
        you saw everywhere left over from the '30s–
the color of the currency no one had–
    in homey wood-handled kitchen tools
or designs inscribed in puddled celadon glaze.
Its Queen Anne cabriole legs
    curve like a mermaid's hip
        slinking down to a tight pinch
    just as the tail might spread its toes on the floor.

My back pressed into the arm of the kitchen couch
    I ache from waist to instep
        with the pulled chemistry of womanhood.
My daughter, eight, reads homework while
    my bent knees form a heelrest
        for her left foot
            which supports
                her right ankle,
                      heel dangling.
Her gymnast fanny warms my feet
    and the old stove hushes
        with the first dinner
            she has ever cooked.
Occasionally she asks about osmosis
    or tells me of the hydras.
Her sniffles are for having our long haired
    cat on her pillow all night long.

Through open windows
        house finches elaborate
                their purling, burry trills.
Certain afternoons sun can angle in,
        loosen some deep muscle
                in thoughts interred for decades,
                      covered over with simple images–
distant roosters, creaking screen door hinge
        that I hear as meadowlark,
or the plain rounded parallels
        of breaking eggs, saving whites.
Every so often a sudden urge
        would capture me, seduce me away
from my desk to whip up an angelfood cake.

And I'd wonder, sometimes, why
        this safety felt so
                long sought, hard won.
Like my father's return after
        so many years at war.
The curve legged stove begins to whisper of his absence.
This one scene I do remember:
        still his silver framed navy portrait
                on the mantel, he'd gather us
        around the dresser size mahogany radio
                to lie on our wool carpet beach
        for the Sundays-at-five show *Hawaii Calls*
hoping its trade winds R&R
        might soothe his family's re-stitched seams,
        as though none of it had ever happened.

The old stove knew of all the years when
        war adopted by grandparents I'd play helper
                amid thick kitchen fragrances
                wet flour, or war rationed sugar, baking.
Knew how I'd watch her pinch a rim of pie dough
        or whip egg whites for angelfood which
                could get tricky. The hardest thing

        was using the whites from turkey eggs,
     so large you had to
          guess at just how much to
          change the proportions of flour and sugar.

In my turn of the century Victorian kitchen
I've replayed how we'd string beans, shell peas, or any other
        produce our neighbor would set on his garden wall,
        re-built on both sides when it would crumble.
I knew even then from the sound the struck rock made
        that it guarded a secret fire
            trapped in its nighted center,
like crystals of love hidden in war's hard geode of shames.
We'd pull pin feathers, singe chickens
          'set the eating-irons out' on the kitchen table
preparing our world for Grandfather's return.

Even now in '70s farmwife skirts on a Tilden path
     I can feel her with me
        see us walk past piles of off-cast river rocks
          to bring him some news,
           or date black-walnut cookies.
Him, king of the
        dirt layered, grinding corrugated metal
three story stair-built square roofed
dredge that dragged up bucket after
        bucket of dripping, glossy mud
          from the brown-red river where it
anchored in search of gold.

And daily we'd walk the path
     in the Mother Lode's fine red dust
        through straw-smelling fields to Millers' barn
          baskets on our arms.
There we exchanged our bread crust custard pudding
        for their butter, eggs, cream and milk,
heard what women told from letters home,

                or news from someone
                back from town
                of planes, a buddy, troops, or FDR.
And the sun reeled out its threads strand after amber strand
           to spin us into positions I'd always repeat.

And every night
           we filled the fresh made mashed potato cups
           with pools of milky gravy.
Papa would sit me across
           the bony girders of his thighs
              his fantastic dignity heated my face with pride.
All the rhythms of my gestures were for them.
He'd tell me made up stories about
           Johnnie And The Pink Cloud, or
still as statues who'd always be gazing like this,
           the amused eagle spangle in his eyes
           glided through the kitchen window
                   over the dryland wheat field
           to hover at some aural source I could not yet make out
but in his deeper, louder minister voice
           he'd say the poems–
              all with words I could not understand
                      but liked best.
And I'd snuggle the scratchy wool of his old man's sweater
           the slippery tie
              scorched smell of his starched shirt.
Even now poems give me pause
           expose a familiar presence.
Their oblique words rouse
           cadences of feeling,
              a phrase delays my certainty,
                      places me in a secret.

Then abruptly screening too many sudden reversals
           the family dammed and submerged
this world– now two worlds lost–
           the house, Camanche town, backyard sandbox and

                    little tin utensils
                              never spoken of,
          her wringer washtub
                    mason jars, the chicken yard, the bounty hawks
                              nailed to fences,
          the thunder-hoofed cattle herds' weekly runs
                    that bullied me wailing
                              from our wide front porch
          as though all the dolls had disappeared
                    the pillows lost their feathers
                                        and the blankets turned to ice.

          And nowadays finally, whenever there is sun
                    my house will almost any hour
                              provide a place to sit in it.
          It has taken me most of my life to order
                              the chairs and couches
                                        in such a way as
                              to absorb and reflect it.

Salvation Painting

Parchment nailed
        like a proclamation
to our moldy sub-basement's
        rough-grained door.
Edged in seeped linseed
        this cobalt and crimson bird
my father painted
        in the stern of a dirt gray tanker
as they sleuthed northward from Kurita's
        for Admiral Ozawa's fleet,
        expecting air attack
                and follow-up battleship fire.

Stretched certain on skinny legs
canary beak strained wide
        insistent on songs
of leafy cliffs, pacific seas
        carmine camellias
        he'll plant back home.
Its sooty eye-dot's tightly focused
        beyond the restless wife
            the daughter sent away,
envisioning gifts
        he'll bring back home
                pearls, and little lacquer bowls.

Indeed the bird sang true,
faced with so much he could not heal
he'd rise at four
        to Brahms before his fireplace,
and Chopin's pastry cadences
        whispered through our house.

Admiral Halsey's Orders

Captain Hansen disobeyed orders
pulled his tanker away from the fleet
knowing enemy pilots would target
oilers to light up the rest of the ships for attack.
At home *Captain Hansen* was said
almost as often as *milk* or *bread* or *shoes*.
When it ended, my dad drove our family
to Long Beach to meet his captain. The kind of
laughing the two of them did
quieted something in me, made life easier.
His hearty wife showed us two 10-inch
tortoises he'd brought her back from somewhere
that now lived under her brick-raised kitchen stove.
For a decade we still heard his name pretty often
and sometimes they'd come north for visits.
But one day Dad came home from his hospital crying,
said they simply sewed the captain up
when they saw his ballooning aorta.
Every so often I finger through
the gold-plated buttons I saved, anchor pins
and ribbons from Dad's uniform
and wonder how many times
I owed my father's return to Captain Hansen.

for Harold "Doc" Golden, Dad's shipmate

Father

Not easy to walk in dry sand
sliding back, compelled to repeat
the same ground toward waves.
Like when you can't say
what it is you mean, words float up
the way pelicans lift broad wings
over a wave crest, drop back again
to glide only inches above the sea.

Listen, the insistent crash, rasp, rustle
a constant lineage of waves
like generations, each folding
spending itself full out upslope
falling, depleted, back on itself
on its own outflow, building
a base for the next.

Gray clouds overhang gray water.
Waves rise up with the urgency
of words, again and again from depths
to ridge, crest, curl,
their felt force

a serious, dark edge,
sharp at the bow
churning white foam at the stern.
Surging from the flat, stretched
backdrop of the cold sea
they come in one after another

as though it was endless
the source of them, so many,
like men from all the small
towns, big cities, rallying across
the seascape, a multitude force.

It was not these waves slipping over
one another, sliding up wet sand
not their solemn spreading
of creamy lace veils, white-hemmed rounds
rounding and rounding
up the glossy beach, that
reminded them of brides back home.

Rather, it was swell after fatal swell
rushing forth to lay themselves down,
waves collapsing upon themselves
willing to spill themselves out
again and again in stringy webs.
It was the waves' fatty sprawling in all
directions across one another,
cold on the steely sand.

Now comes a long legged
Marbled Godwit, tentative, solitary being
standing, looking, reaching deeper, her long
and slightly upturned bill
probes the wave-brought mud from the sea,
scrivening strings of holes
meandering cursive lines
of stories scrolled out in foreign
symbols, signs. The unspoken language
scrawled all along night's waterline
again and again, the waves' long sentences
letters to living descendants
the tales my father refused to tell.
"It was all a bad dream." But I'd hear him
often scream in his sleep, turbulent
ships in cold seas.

Purple medals the khaki bluffs,
and offshore brown, dark
ridge-backed bulls of outcrop rock

stand as survivors of storms' onslaughts.
White, rounded breasts of a hundred
hunched gulls face north in
early stillness. Fog obscures
mountain outlines dropping to the sea.
Car lights curve the road to work.
Surfers in black rubber wet suits
wait in foam to ride on the backs of
those gray ships.

Right Relation

The sting, the slap as ocean hits my skin
like ice held to a wound, or the slicing snap
of leather. Tight strain
of bicep, shoulder against surf
each driving stroke
pulls away from what the body
knows by heart. Under the surface
Kailua Bay's thalo shadows
signal submerged blocks,
broken sea wall. Anchor chains,
long buried, shed rust.
Pulling away from breakers behind
in tomboy stance designed
to disguise my oldest stain,
skin like seaweed
clumped on cold gray sand.
Pulling away from the discourse
of some other, her cipher
sealed in my flesh.

But, there, the turtle
hovering over rocks
in the waves' soft rise and drop,
and nearly a dozen lemon tangs
picking at strands of green and purple *limu*
growing on her brown, domed shell,
ribbons of *limu* flowing like hair.
We hung there in the encircling sea
like yellow words said over and over,
become sound only,
gazing, invisible at last.
There in the rocking surge I realized
the gasp that comes with sudden wonder
cleanses us to our very bones
parts us from others' cruelties,

which after it all are only about themselves,
starts us off anew again
like Grandmother's large hand
pressing my head to her chest
when she would say *There, there...*
Which really meant *Here. Here.*

Serpent in the River

Heavy river, deep wide rapids
gray-beige silted two-foot waves.
A bark canoe is riding high
a tall man calmly stroking downstream.

Proudly smiling sitting upfront
white-veiled broad hat, satin gowned
height of femininity
my grandmother, his bride.

A serpent's many backs are rising
from the water's depths beside them.
All around, its thick brown body
undulates, as large as they are
swimming down through crests fast moving
staying alongside of them.

I am fearful for their safety
but they beam their wedding pride.
It is the river of their dying,
Papa now has come for her
as in her dreams she saw he would.

10/14/80 10:15 am

Thick sharp smells of homemade soap
    of sun dried laundry
        the iron on clean clothes
    of fresh-made beds
        the house clean throughout.
Years of roses, ripe fruits
    of new dough's flour and yeast aromas
    of air and sunshine, a house rich with visiting.
Her maternal drone interested, hearing inevitabilities
    bright response to a good piece of news,
        Oh dear, oh my yes, telling facts, confirming.
Acceptance, reality. This is the way things are.
    Take care of everything and keep
        everything the way it is supposed to be.
Yes? Yes? Um hmmm. Oh, my dear, yes.
A strange, overwhelming sleepiness
    would for years after I was married
        overcome me as I entered her house
positioning the past nearer to dreams.
    I was healthy but she was
    to me more alive
        than I, I ashamed and thought
that it meant I didn't like
    to be with her as much as
    my dear yes, I wanted. A nap? A nap?
You just got here my dear, what ever a nap is wrong with you?

And her silver brooches, the engraved
    gold buckle brooch with thin curved teeth
her sapphire set in platinum filigree
    that her husband gave her
    that I saw pinned to the bosom of her dress
        almost every day
    that I wore on my wedding gown, and
    that was lost for some years and was found again.

Round black-walnut cutting board
      hewn by her father when she married Papa.
In Penn Valley to visit a grave together
      under huge oaks, her mother, her grandmother?
Hot dry grasses hiding cicadas and framing
      wild tiger lilies, orange and native and tall.

The pan for grating soap in
      the knives sharper even than Dad's,
            her silver pill box.
The gnarled knuckles
      fingers interlaced loosely on her lap
      thumbs circling one another
      shiny round fingernails
      the cardboard manicure box
the shaking throat skin, the curling chin hairs, the wax.
The way her mouth
      stretched into plump cheeks
            in chuckling smiles and shaking laughter
            hands still folded.
The pinkish lenses of her glasses, the combs
      she pushed into her rolled hairline, hair nets.

Roses, huge and fragrant in sun-bright
      crystal bowls on the desk by the wall of windows.
Always the same things in drawers
      everything that's supposed to be
            but no clutter, nothing unneeded.
Always she sent me home with armloads of clean laundry
      a few new hand towels
          a pressure cooker I could use
      and magazine clippings she knew I would be needing.

Earlier, red coffee cans filled with bacon fat
      would sit on our counter
            till there were six of them
            or three, if her neighbor
            had two, and Grandmother one.

And when we would visit we would take them to her
        and it would take three or six days
                and we couldn't watch
                      (lye was dangerous)
and she transformed grease
        into the white smooth soap which Papa
                would cut and grate in the basement
and give back again to whomever might want to be using it.

And later, others would grate the soap
        and then it wasn't used so much anymore.
And she hardly ever arrived or left our house
        without baking boxes of date-nut cookies
                always the same, dream inducing
with homely pockets of flour
                cupped against the dates or nuts.
And years later I could tell
        when it was hard for her to mix anymore.
The cookies would be oily or brittle
        or granular, or too floury.

Jars washed and saved on shelves
        in her basement where her neighbor parked his car.
Going to town on the streetcar
        setting the eating irons on the table
                using real butter, not smear
                      a little rich milk poured over dessert.
Moving slowly, but always moving
        her constant going into the next moments
and never very far at once
        but always firmly moving this day along into the next.

Ghost Pines

Transparent ghostly
      gray-green guardians
           vague silent presences
                lacy, shiny needles,
soft ascetic spirits of the mountainside
      uttering among themselves
           high harmonic tones of protection
                earthward pull
my elderly grandparents.

Meadowlarks

Their eerie unexpected celestial ring
    chills the full space
        of permanent silence,
the eternally wavering radiance
    of dry flat grasslands
        at Brown's Valley
where my grandmother's grandmother
        quavered in giving birth.
The long hair of the earth
    shivers forth the cries
of meadowlarks across the dimpled body
    of California foothills
and into the still heat of midday.

        Kahakai, Huaka'ipo
            across Hualālai's Kaupulehu flow

Final days of my mother's fitful life
      I happen to be walking
the *path of deceased spirits*
           on part of the ancient Ala Loa
                along Kaupulehu Bay.
Salty vapor bakes off rounded lava
waves wash turtles
      sighing in their sleep.
Sea breeze flicks my face and hair
      teases the skirt
           against my thighs.
Wind's twin mantras
      lift a lifetime's fears away.
Oh, rattle your palms, you zephyrs of the spirit
      and take my harshness with you, wind.
Forgive my hiding, reluctances, retreats
        scrub our hearts of others' faults.
Rinse from the sands of my flesh the signs
      and bring me back my words.
Signs bid us *ho'omaha li'ili'i*
           rest a little
along the Kahakai huaka'ipo.

Seed-crystal magnets
         to gather peaceful memories
amulets against night marchers:
my father at his fireplace
     pre-dawn reading in his chair
or in his garden toiling out
     his soul's alchemy.
          Ho'omaha li'ili'i
rest a little, now and again.

Waves receding
        down the cove's sloped shore
clatter applause
        from rolling cobbled rocks.

Other

Three hours alone
    in your presence
        nothing still,
your lips pursed as before.
But my words too
   have always plunged
back into that leaden
   blistered bone beneath my breath.
I leave you now
   heart emptying.
Ah, the sun, Ohio breeze
how lovely that house
   soft the grass.
A mourning dove
   a robin's call.
Write these down
   on yellow post-it,
start the purple rental car.

Áumākua

Had I really gone that fast?
Of the complete stop I didn't
              need reminding
there at the crest, the short drop
to the national downhill finish
and all their yelling in the frozen wind.
Coach said indeed I had been
              headed for first
no longer scared of the icy speed.
We all laughed.
Years later when you held me–
footfalls echo peaches' milky fragrance–
my blood raced. But you teased, and
too quickly again I misperceived
              misconstrued everything.
Everything.   And now, this boulder.
A shadow said it wasn't there by chance
its pore-pocked surface, lengthwise crack
were holding something for me.
The hatchet angle of some ancient profile
              drew me into question.
I'd gaze and wonder who this presence was.
Then the head line, slope of nose
were dipping to the ocean floor
yanking bits of *limu* from the lava,
rocked in surge, domed shell lifted upwards.
Swimming beside I've yearned for it to lift me.
The sea lifts and drops us, lifts and drops.
The hooded eye meets mine, steady, unafraid
unmoved by my spirit's expenses, my insignificance.

At Starr's Place

Starr loved the army jeep I learned to drive in
        that Dad bought for my brothers to dismantle.
He'd take us on day trips along Sierra fire roads,
        one she later drove three times to scatter
            half my family's ashes
        into a lake he chose.

Starr took me to a mountaintop to show me
a mile wide windblown molecule—
        acres of atoms in frenzied oscillation—
the white-dusted slopeside was lathered in wild parsley's
        shaking stamen dots
            held high above each splash
                of tiny ivory flowerlets
as though our sister Artemis
        reached down to stir her bath suds.

We found some sticky wild currant leaves
        whose spicy fragrance was my father's ritual,
            we'd always squeeze their leaves
                in walking past.
His garden was his palace and camellias were its prize.
Names come back in syllables rolling like finch songs
        Camellia japonica, Kumasaka, Debutante,
        Oenethera, Primula malcoides, Heuchera micrantha.

Jeeping and hiking in marshy meadows
we came upon wild-haired sky-eyed Art
        who studied butterflies
        who talked of reciprocity,
            "And therein lies an interesting tale."
He said those small blue alpine butterflies
        lay their eggs on certain plants
            from which the ants

                    carry them underground.
Feeding these butterfly larvae
        with their own ant eggs,
the ants then suckle honey from
        the caterpillars' skin
              at glands the learnèd say evolved
              to serve this symbiotic purpose.
And finally when the pupal form matures
it readies for emergence from the nest
        forming waxy scales over its body
          easing the climb to sunshine and to flight,
but also as armor against their hosts'
            biting to impede their moving on.

That evening on her granite boulder porch
we sip and chat and listen
        fox sparrows whistle, juncos trill
        finches sing coloraturas.
Above the understory of breeze-shifting ferns
      rise shocking re-curved orange tiger lilies,
and flies spiral like gems refracting
        in light shafts slanting through the firs.

Louisa

Decades later I finally learned
my hard-working tiny grandmother
searched six years for a lawyer
who would take her case
for divorce.
Though she'd helped two
sons through med school
her struggles were hidden,
only stories of her popular
restaurant cooking,
business sense,
her humor.
Times in my life I needed more
to know of her strength
when my hard work felt
only like my father.
But recalling her too infrequent visits
busily cooking and cleaning our messy kitchen
or studying the newspaper,
sometimes she'd press her
neatly groomed hand on my forearm
and she'd speak in heavy accent of my future,
her brightly focused eyes
her mysterious intensity
reached deep in my mind
lovingly breathed her wry smiling certitude
past a war torn
smokescreen generation into mine.

Migration

Today, our spring is dry, the creek
        empty
                edges us out again.
The chill lake echoes
        underbrush reddening
                fiery towards downfall.
Departing bushtits,
        hundreds, lilt with chickadees
        through dry arbor.
Ruddy ducks
        congregate, exhausted.
        Heads under wing by sundown
                they lift away at dawn.

Today. Last visit
        with my Aunt Lilly?
        Every fall I feel this
now she's ninety-five.
Large blue honest eyes
        steady my heart to her task.
Our arms around
        each other like girls
        in autumn's veil
of thinning light–
        the distance blurs,
        my edges soften,
                give over.

Prayer

Rest well, thou dearest part
   of who I was.
Draw saffron finches
  to your grass seeds.
Let the jacaranda roots
  lift you to her branches
to feed and harbor
  myriad insects
    for foraging warblers,
shelter monarch
  butterflies at night.

Throughout the day my cardinal friend
  will call to you
    naming the sites of our village.
Your sister moon
  will arc her path above you
    in our unwavering dialogue.
Pray, make another place for me
  in the streaming
    thrusts of substance
      through this earth.

Part V

The Eleventh

The Eleventh

Stark airliner silhouette
                        blue September morning sky
                                              silver buildings
no possible
            transition
                        the New American Century's
first   Daemonic Apocalypse
orange volcanic   billows foam   Death redoubled
      pour down   Bone Deep   Dread
                to Loom among us.

Decades' Exponential Hatred,   its
                  Aweful rapture of Requital,   its
                                    numinous Moral
Exaltation.
What were they thinking of God?   Of Divine Justice?
                  No Other
                          Means?
This strangely hidden   Mystery of Nature (human)
                  broke through
      our Complacent republic.

As its Shadow crossed our nation
                we all Saw
                          began   Losing
                                    Everything.
Then quietly
        across parking lots
                Love Spread
                      playgrounds
                            coffee shops
                                  filling stations.
Humble, Grateful
        a grandson's sweaty hand
                a secure mortgage,   or work,
                                  or a friend.

    Our eyes meet
            our Nulled selves touch
                          we keep Listening
Names drift west in the Nothingness of our Ashes

            Lord help us   Lord help us
a Presence felt in the dark
            Because Unseen
                    only a way to try to say It.
Our gravid Stillness steadies
                to newly Broken Open
        Vision.
Maybe marks the Start of
        Readiness to
                Question.

          9-13-01, my grandson's fifth birthday

Too Big To Jail

Say,   and   Do: AnyThing,
   No Fear
Use insider info
   without getting   caught
Derive opaque devices
that'll   easily   slide right past
 any Government Regulation.

Triumph of Language
     Over Truth:
Alt-A   was just   what they called
crappy   mortgage loans   for which
they   hadn't   even   bothered to
verify   the borrower's   income.
Distressed districts "are OK, Now!"

And   *a bond   backed entirely*
by   sub-prime   mortgages
  (for example)
 Wasn't   called a   Sub-Prime
  Mortgage Bond.
It   was called   an   ABS,
Or: Asset   Backed   Security.

CDO
In a CDO you gather   thousands
of the country's   Worst mortgages
call   the batch   'Diversified'   and
Re-rate   80% of it   as triple-A.
A Simple way   to launder   Simple
folks' Terrible credit, and   soon
to   Throw   Them   Out,
  But   Turn
Wall Street   Lead   into   Gold.

(Pre-)Algebra
Hmm. Let's see. If you have
Valued a bond assuming 10%
Is the X-number of
  Sub-Prime contents,
What Would its Value be
If X is *really* 95%. ??

More Advanced (8th graders only)
The Problem:
A double-A slice of a CDO
  costs   0.5%/yr;
A triple-B slice costs 2%.
Which is a better bet?
The Answer:
Since we know
  the   pie's   the   same
   throughout
You can buy a bet *against* it
Four Times Bigger
If you buy at 0.5%.

Too Big To Fail
These bonds renamed as Triple-A
 THE-Oh!-RE-TI-CAL-LY
   could then be sold to
companies who were
  allowed to invest   Only–
ONLY– in highly rated   securities
you know,   the Funds which
Hold Our Futures
   in   their hands.

So, Wall Street's *Shadow Banks*
  gone to the dark side
sold them *as foolproof,*
  impervious to loss.
Sold them to:
  -German banks
  -Taiwanese insurance firms
  -Japanese farmers' unions
  -European pension funds
and to savings banks, credit unions,
commercial banks, pension funds,
  unions, insurance funds
in nearly Every Nation All Around
The World–
World Trade? "*The World Wonders.*"
That's right, to funds meant to secure
Everyone's Retirement,
  health care, investments
  auto and fire insurance

local school funds,
(by now you can fill this out for yourself
and See where you and your children and
their children and your parents and your
neighbors and *other countries* Fit In).

And then, Guess What?   Then,
after They'd sold them as foolproof
Then They   had   More Cash
To Make More New Home Loans
        to yet more folks who
never could repay adjusted rates.

Synthetics
Do you think synthetic stuff tastes bad?
Try A Bit Of This:
They made a CDS–
        an i*nsurance contract between*
an investment bank *(uh huh, Shadow)*
        and some other bank
            or insurance company
to hedge,   to protect   *Themselves*
against a loss of value in
        Their   CDOs
you know, that cross-section of
        adjustable rate mortgages
        the really insecure ones.
And   Then   They figured out
They could simply
        take one step over into
            The Wild Side
and buy these CDSs *Themselves*
without even *owning* the CDO.
Like you buying insurance on
            your neighbor's house.
Well *Then, That's* when
        the grass really caught fire.
When They–
    The Shadow Banks–
could really get Their (Bonus) Bang
            for Your Buck.

For $25 Million A Year Salary:
Betting Against "Their Own."

And   They   Placed   Bets
        On/For/and Against
every   unthinkable   position.
And *Then* They
        invented, "synthesized" CDSs
        custom-made for Themselves,
with enough fine print to hide the fact of an insurance payoff to themselves proportionate to the full amount of the price of a brand new house even in the case of only a broken window, And dead certain to pay off.

The Best and the Brightest
        <Math Students in America??>
*Nope, Wall Street Traders are
        quitting
Their big firms to work at
Hedge funds, where they can make*
        <A Difference, you hope??>
Nope, *not tens but*
        Hundreds of Millions.

Freely Enterprising
And, a few clever investors, like L Figured:
        Figured Out that IF...
  IF:: AIG, the CDOs' major buyer,
sniffed the CDOs' fragile nature,
    and quit buying them:: Then,
*the entire subprime mortgage
        bond market might collapse...
and L's Credit Default Swaps
        would be worth a fortune....*
L flew to London– (World Trade)–
to try to Make That Happen.
Whereupon the end owner
        of the CDO receives
            a little note, "We regret..."

The ARMs Re-Set
from their teaser rates
            to higher rates.

The "Owners" learned they
        couldn't afford them after all
and they lost the house
        the lenders said they could.
Then the various bonds
that THE SHADOW BANKS made
        from those loans went bad
and so did the CDSs
They made from the bonds.
Here's where *THE FEW*
        swept the poker chips
        into *Their* bags
making a fortune exploiting
        Congress' loopholes
in: The Newly *De-Regulated*
        American Century.

How Do You Explain
To an innocent citizen
of the free world
the importance of
a credit default swap
on a double-A tranche
of a sub-prime backed
collateralized debt obligation?

One: AIG had sold "insurance"–
bets–
    ("in case" borrowers defaulted)
      to every major financial firm
in the World. Yes, in the
    Entire World, nearly every
major financial firm bought
insurance (to Trade Away Risk)
against complex *SHADOW BANK*
"products" no one understood.
    Around the World
They'd slithered tentacles
between and into all of the World's
    financial systems, operations,
      Trades, Bloodstream.
Two: Then all at once
  Banks Quit Trading Cash for
Houses-Split-All-Ends-up
Chopped and re-Pasted like Plywood
in Wall Street's mill into stocks.

THE TOWERS of Matchsticks
Failed. Collapsed. Rapidly.

Three: When banks
      stopped lending
credit stopped Trade stopped
businesses couldn't produce,
employees got laid off, teachers
    policemen, transit workers
hospitals ran out of medicine.

Which is why We were told that
We had to buy *Their* failures out,
If *They* went down, We all might.

The International Monetary Fund
gauged losses created by
      American *"Financiers"*
at a Trillion dollars.
      One Trillion Dollars
            In Losses.
    All Around the World.
That's right, in Funds meant to
Secure Everybody's Future.
Losses Embedded in
      Everybody's Households in
the president's Ownership Society.
Losses hidden away in all those loans
on houses Suddenly Worth only Half
    what *They* said they were.
    Losses Snaked Out of
Everyone's retirement accounts,
    plans, hopes.
Embedded: *They* sleep, We don't.
Embedded in almost Every
      lower- and middle-class
Household In The World.
And also them as don't have
    Houses anymore.

Boat For Sale

13 foot wood boat.
this is a project
boat that would bee a
neat father son hobby.
it come with trailer.
bought it for same
purpose for
me and my son but
things happen
and now we
have to move.
so need to get
rid of it! first on
with the money
gets it.
wont last long!!!

Part VI
Notes

Preface

> "Poetry is...," John Stuart Mill

Part I- Hatch Reflection

> "The Mirror of Eternity":
> Eternity is not the mirror, but the reflected.
> Victor White on Aquinas' *in speculo aeternitatis.*
> <u>God and the Unconscious</u>

"Hatch Reflection"
Grace Works *Through* Nature
    Aquinas joined the Order of Preachers in order to combat the argument that matter, the body, and worldly realities were bad, sinful (as opposed to spiritual vision which was good, holy). This negative position was known as Albigensian Gnosticism. Thomas' goal was the unveiling of humans' ultimate significance, and their guidance through time toward eternity.
    Aquinas' main theological premise in this regard is that Grace Works *Through* Nature, within matter and according to the natural law. God works in the physical world and through the body, which is inherently good. In fact he states that earthly concerns, sexuality, and extravert activity, if at the service of charity, may be of more eternal worth than the spiritual perceptions themselves.

"Hatch Reflection" Angelology!
    "Thomas (Aquinas) is at great pains to give the important theological idea of 'angelic enlightenment' a rational basis. He categorically denies that Old Testament revelation was ever the effect of immediate Divine agency. Of Acts vii. 53 and Galatians iii. and Epistle to the Hebrews he says that the Old Law was mediated by angels (I-II. 98. 3.*) And in sharp contradiction to St Albert the Great and many medieval Christian and Jewish divines, Thomas asserted the identity of the 'angels' of the Scripture with the immaterial, separated 'intelligences' of metaphysical speculation. The very name 'angel' indicates a *function* rather than a substance. (In Matt. xv. I.) Such functions are contemplation, or mediating the unknown to consciousness, or intellectual strengthening.

(I. 108. 2 and 5.*) They do not overrule the ordinary processes of psychology and biology, but work in and through matter, employing its resources and obeying its laws. In Thomas' mind the proximate and immediate causes of supernatural prophesy were invariably biological or physical in character."
from Victor White, God and The Unconscious
*Thomas Aquinas, Summa Theologica

"Mona Lisa," "Fire Poem"
  As with people, the natural objects in our lives are not inert, but have a dynamic presence which draws us in various ways into relation with our reality, forming a continuous silent dialogue. Through a developed sense of the significance of the objects in our lives (objects being people, natural beings, constructed objects, patterns of culture, anything) we can accomplish the mind's task of retrieving lost spiritual forms and energies in our perceptions of the phenomenal world.
  In the last two decades (and for my husband, actually six), we have read the pain of the forests in the many very serious fires that have raged through the Cascades region that we have come to know so intimately. Devotion to the forests and oceans as brothers, though really they are mirrors, can lead us in ethical valuations, *e.g.* to stop growing rice where cotton should be, and to stop growing cotton where un-irrigated pasture should be. By now, most of us have become aware of what is needed.
  Added note: Indeed the lakeside stand of lodgepole pines in "Mona Lisa" had been blighted by pine beetle, were entirely brown when we left the lake last autumn, and had been removed by the Forest Service by the time we returned late this spring. One can no longer observe the light pattern phenomenon described in the poem.

"The Pink Cricket"
Grace Works Through Nature
  The imagination selects, combines, and forms sense impressions in its own way, in imaginary space and time, and not necessarily according to the known patterns of the 'outer world'.
  Through its ability to present the mind with images of the absent, the possible and the future, it is the imagination supremely which constellates emotions, goals, dangers, patterns of culture.
  Also, the imagination often produces images of whose origin the subject is unconscious. What happens when we say that God reveals, is precisely the psychological occurrence in a person's

mind, their vision, their awareness of what is commonly hidden from human perception. We might say that through direct perception this person sees what is opaque to average consciousness.

So for Aquinas, the imagination would be the vehicle for conveyance of knowledge over and above what people might discover by the directed employment of their own sense and intelligence. The images seen in this way, then, are not mere *signs* for what is otherwise knowable, but true *symbols* of meaning, significance: symbols for what wholly transcends sense perception or rational comprehension, but that reveal conclusions regarding humanity's ultimate purposes and meaning, eternity, if you will.

What some might call revelation and prophesy, along with Aquinas, are a certain kind of consciousness, a cognitive psychological event, remote from ordinary vision. It is an inward vision consisting of concrete images, often brought about in a state of solitude or introversion. The mere perception of an occurrence is not a revelation, but rather the outcome of the occurrence's significance for their guidance (or guidance of humanity) in terms of eternal design. Though momentarily undergone, it is not something that the recipient does, but that is perceived as being done to them, that overpowers them.

Psychological discernment of the subject's reality orientation and motive is always relevant to the interpretation of the images and conclusions. Revelation is often more concerned with what people imagine than with precision of statement about the external world. In its most typical forms revelation is indistinct and unclear, everything of which the controlled, orderly, logical and scientific reason is most suspicious. But the cultural significance of the symbols themselves may indeed remain indisputable.

Aquinas' understanding, then, is that God penetrates the mind through the imagination as the vehicle of revelation.

"Boat Train"

"Whose spirit is this?" i.e. Where does this spirit (of song and gazing enchantment) come from, and what function does it serve (in this context, for these girls)? And for us who enjoy the songs (or poems) as well?

Joseph Campbell has said the central myth of our time is the Planet. And that to take as our central myth of valuation and security the purity of earth's winds and waters is no less culturally challenging than the stoic acceptance of living without a God. This latter would be the 20th century task implied in Stevens' poem where the singer's own imaginings create her sensed order, rather than a received spirit from a divine source. Countering past centurys' anthropomorphized or romanticized nature portrayals of God's immanence, Stevens' nature is stripped down, not consoling. But he does strive to in some way contain, integrate those experiences which used to be comfortably attributed to theological principles.

Mircea Eliade describes myths as functioning to situate a culture meaningfully in time and space. They describe to us the models by which we order our values and significance, recognize the purposes of life, agree to permissions and injunctions. Myth also articulates for us how our life fits into a larger pattern of the eternal radiating through the present, enables us to recognize a sense of accord with the universe (surroundings, people, whatever constitutes our context), thereby achieving harmony and reconciliation, countering a merely profane perspective of anesthetized indifference, alienation.

Campbell actually describes this experience of accord with humanity and the universe as the ultimate religious experience. (In Christian terms this would be the beatific vision, connecting us not only with our environment and humanity, but with divine presence as well). And Stevens, in different language, describes such bonds: "these are the measures destined for their souls"; "Not just...moods in falling snow, but falling snow itself "; "Sweet land," "Cherished like the thought of heaven, but the reality of heaven, eternity itself." These are expressions of wonder at physical phenomena, and a kind of faith investment in the earth itself for support.

The particular oneness I observed in my summertime neighbors appeared to be achieved through a transitional substitution in the mind: the earth becomes that supportive, containing, enchanting figure from earliest consciousness, and the passion of faith in the Other is re-invested in earth. The girls, in their floating chain of containments and attachments, show us what it looks like to experience Planet Earth (lake, forest, mountain, wind, rain, sun, creatures) as a sustaining reliability that functions like a divinity.

"Scrap Metal"
       italics from Heidegger and Shakespeare

"Bright *Thou*"

Duet songs and dances maintain a pair bond until environmental conditions are right for breeding, thereby losing no time searching for a mate.

"...The bright *Thou* appeared and was gone" was Martin Buber's description of the brevity of moments in our relations when true address receives true response. In dynamic relatedness the intensity of focus can be experienced as so vital that the individuality of the participants fades, the threshold of separateness seems transcended. But Buber observes that this is not unity. "The immediacy of relation cannot persist... everything is destined to re-enter the condition of objects...The unreliable, perilous world of relation...has no density, or duration.." What Buber calls the I/Thou relation consists solely in the immediacy of this primal meeting.

The significance of the natural world is that its mysteries are lived without escaping the paradox of these irreconcilable propositions of presence and absence. Our interest awakens when something approaches us, comes to meet us in nature. The mockingbird moves from a secure distance of primitive disinterestedness to a quality of inquiry and brief relation or recognition of the other in the form of a gaze. We know only our part, not the other's, though we strain towards it. Their part we only experience in the meeting, and only for the space of a glance.

And so, to whom am I the bird? Most important in Buber's view is the relation to God. In theological terms only one Thou never ceases to be present. It is only we who are not always there, due to the unconsciousness which normally envelops our own minds.

"Standing Amidst Bats"

Nature so often rivets our attention and gives us a vocabulary of images in which to analogize our metaphysical and religious ideas. Perceptual experiences in nature can call us up sharply to pay closer heed to some issue that has lingered just beneath the threshold of conscious awareness. But nature does not provide a direct path to the knowledge about an ultimate Being, nor can it sanctify us. Nature can give us parallels for the theories we already hold, can stimulate doubt or questions, fill out a sense of glory or of faith.

Nature's language can illuminate, represent, bring felt meaning to concepts like wonder, glory, humility, mercy, terror, hope, purity, but it cannot teach us theological principles. These we must bring *to* our experiences in nature. We must learn them elsewhere, and then understand more fully the significance of those concepts as incarnated in wilderness, ocean, farmland, city parks, backyards.

"Bruddaman"

The classic epistemological 'problem of other minds' is the determination of whether gestures and behaviors arise from genuine mental states, and are therefore the conscious, thinking products of 'another mind.' Regularity of the action in response to stimuli would justify such an inference. The operational definition would measure appropriateness of the creature's behavior as indication of conscious, sentient, intelligent being. Most of us have observed our animals to be furiously active theorizers, and it is conventional wisdom that pigs are pretty smart.

Our own human common-sense conception of the world results from a process of conceptual development and learned discrimination that parallels our apprehension and anticipation of the world. We consider our ability to make useful introspective discriminations as the outcome of long neuro-physiological evolution, as success in making predictively useful judgments and explanatory theories of our environments. In <u>The Future of Man</u>, Teilhard de Chardin defines "reflective purposiveness, slowly acquired" as the capacity by which life can develop in the twofold direction of greater complexity and fuller consciousness.

It is probably inaccurate to say Bruddaman would not have faced the same complexity of discriminations had his mother survived to rear him in the wild. And probably we cannot apply the concept of the human raised pig as becoming more evolutionarily advanced. Rather we can say that we have a context in which to understand the conceptual capacities of his species because we have noticed parallels to our own cognitive behaviors and their underlying assumptions.

"Mauna Kea Silverswords"
See The Hawaiian Journal Of History, volume 45; 2011 for an introduction to the cultural divide over placement of telescopes on Mauna Kea.

Briefly, this is a culturally sacred mountaintop where unique atmospheric and topographic conditions (reaching above 40% of earth's atmosphere) were recognized in the 1960s as presenting an unusual opportunity for astronomy research. Broken trust between scientific and indigenous cultures has led to a call for limits to expansion of astronomy industrial development in the uniquely fragile environment and sacred landscape. Similar conflicts have arisen at Mount Graham, Arizona.

Mauna Kea is the site of the creation story for the Hawaiian Islands, steeped in heritage and spirituality. It is part of a cultural landscape that has for centuries held religious significance across the Hawaiian Islands and Polynesia. The summit area is the sacred realm, *wahi pana*, where divine entities lived, and people did not. It is a burial ground embodying the Hawaiian gods and the most sacred ancestors. In being denied access to the site, indigenous peoples feel they have been deprived of many important ritual practices.

The Hawaiian cultural conflict has been manifested in long held resentment of the US overthrow of the Hawaiian government in 1893, their annexation, with 25% of lands ceded to the US government, and the suppression of their language. (For all of which the US Congress issued a formal apology signed by President Clinton in 1993.)

The conflict is deeply charged by native-born residents' low economic security. The economy of Hawaii is largely dependent on tourism and US military presence; as a result, a large percentage of residents experience inadequate employment and medical care. Land and housing speculation has rendered a very great many native islanders unable to buy their homes. Hawaii's public education ranks nearly the lowest in the country despite what I've been told is the largest DOE administrative staffing in America.

"Whale"

Christopher M. Dewees, Wick Award Sea Grant scientist, Gyotaku Master. Coincidentally, Dr. Dewees is a fifth generation nephew of Immanuel Kant, some of whose ideas are utilized in this poem. Grant and Katai Anderson were skippers of the vessel *Rocky*. A third skipper from the Bodega Bay Salmon Fleet, Jim Hie, was the photographer and brought the story to me as well as an article from the newspaper, *Bodega Bay Navigator*.

The opening stanza is composed mostly of irresistible excerpts from Melville's <u>Moby Dick</u>, which set the scene and ask the questions relevant to my poem. The outcome of Ahab's whale encounters stems from (what *I* read to be) his position of intense and defining anger at God's remoteness and abandonment of humanity. The whale has clearly changed its meaning in my poem, as has the protagonists' answer to Melville's question. The progression of my "Whale" characters from their experience of the *Mysterium Tremendum* at first as terror and dread, then through awe-struck wonder to baptism, salvation, and renewal is premised upon their outlook beginning with a withdrawal from community similar to Ahab's, but influenced by *"some instilled notion"* out of which their receptivity and responsiveness arise.

Kant describes this indwelling as *"the treasure buried in the field of obscure ideas, constituting the deep abyss of human knowledge, which we cannot sound."* (Lectures on Psychology, Liepzig ed., 1889.) He speaks of a hidden substantive source from which religious ideas and feelings are formed, which lies in the mind independently of sense experience, a 'pure reason' in the profoundest sense, higher than theory and practical reason. Aquinas defines the source of spiritual growth as a hidden 'predisposition' of the human spirit, awakened into the stage he calls *'prevenient grace'*: this state of mind is a longing and searching beyond created things for an unknown that draws the heart and soul.

The essence of religion is the very idea of holiness, sacredness, transcendent value. The fisher characters' capacity of deeply absorbed contemplation when confronted by the vast, living totality of things becomes their preparation for the numinous, their capacity for the recognition of holiness, the intuition of the eternal in the temporal. In the development of religious consciousness, curious phenomena often capture the imagination. Natural objects, whether frightful or extraordinary, arouse a sense of sympathetic rapport between people and their objects.

Their importance is the glimpse of an eternal in and beyond the temporal and penetrating it, the apprehension of a ground and meaning of things in and beyond the empirical and transcending it, *"intimations of meanings figuratively apprehended."** An obscure idea and basis of meaning rises into greater clarity, begins to form the notion, however vague and fleeting, hesitant (*'haunting'*), of a transcendent something, an operative entity from beyond the borders of natural experience. The objective world becomes a reality fraught with mystery and momentousness. For Christians the revelation of the *mystery* of Christ is the interior perception of the meaning (the making *real* of the *symbol* in its outward embodiment) in the eternal designs of God.

- *'not-unfolded'* and 'unexplicated concepts' are Kant's phrases to denote obscure, dim principles which must be felt and cannot be stated explicitly as premises, not worked out in accordance with a clear intellectual scheme.
- *'labyrinthine pathways'* comes from Goethe.
- *'break the rounded unity'* (of the assumptions received from conventional wisdom), rising up from the deeps below consciousness pointing to a unity of a higher order. (The italicized phrase is from Melville)
- *Poseidon's Grove*: remotely distant, profound silence, calm stillness, sacramental silence.

Further references:
* (Rudolf Otto paraphrasing Schleiermacher's <u>Discourses on Religion</u>, *1799).*
Rudolf Otto, <u>The Idea Of The Holy</u>
Victor White, <u>God and The Unconscious</u>

Part II- *Tell Them About The Trees*

"Tell Them About The Trees"
    "Tithonus" by Tennyson is the source of one of my favorite stanzas, this one so settled in its measure of life:
    "The woods decay, the woods decay and fall.
    The vapours weep their burthen to the ground.
    Man comes and tills the field and lies beneath,
    and after many a summer dies the swan."

Horace's poem is "The Anniversary"

"Bill"
    The Laocoön reference in this poem is to to the classic depiction of physical struggle in the heart-rending 1st century sculpture of the Trojan priest and his two sons fighting against serpents sent by Athena (though some claim Poseidon, some Apollo) as protector of the Greeks during the Trojan War, to punish

him for attempting to warn the Trojans of the wooden horse peace prize actually hiding war-armed Greeks. Google it. It's remarkable. This is the same reference made to Laocoön in "Whale."

"MRI"
quote from "*Falling Asleep Over <u>The Aeneid,</u>*" by Robert Lowell

"Ariadne's Threads"
     In the philosophy of logic, Ariadne's Thread refers to a practice of keeping some sort of record of all proposed and attempted solutions to a question, especially incorrect solutions. This allows one to backtrack to a point at which one was correct, and to proceed with further attempts from that point. Not nearly as highly regarded for problem solving as deductive reasoning. But, it can often be the basis for what we call common sense or pragmatism, which are not necessarily severely skeptical.

Part III- Treading Pu'u O'o

"I-80," "Treading Pu'u O'o" and "Pu'u Loa Petryoglyphs":
     These poems refer to three very different forms of visible lava, the first being an open lake of molten lava, bubbling and slowly swirling, its solidifying plates crushing one another back into the orange pool. This is how people were able to view Halema'uma'u in the 19th century, though there were only a few days at a time spread over the 20th century when this was possible. We were lucky enough to be at Kīlauea on one of these rare days. The second form of lava is the smooth, wavy, crusted pāhoehoe produced by a fast flow (pronounced pah-hoy-hoy). The third is the a'ā which is sharp, chunky, usually impossible to walk over because it is so broken and piled up, due to hardening as it flows so slowly.
     The only alternative to the vulnerability of loving is to become unbreakable, impenetrable, like the a'ā.
     Heiau is the term for a shrine devoted to a specific function or identity. The word serves as both singular and plural (pronounced hay-ee-ow).
     Nāmakaokaha'i of the sea who tormented her sister Pele of the earth's fire: Are these goddesses any less believable than a virgin who gives birth to the son of God?

"Aquinas' Logic and MH's"
   quote from Rudolf Otto, The Idea of the Holy, Oxford University Press.

"D.C. Poem"
   Quaternity images emerge in times of psychic turmoil and convey a sense of stability and rest. The image of the fourfold nature of the psyche provides stabilizing orientation. It gives one a glimpse of static eternity. For elaboration see: Edward Edinger, Ego and Archetype

"Just what is the evil..." quote from David Simpson, 9/11

Part IV- *Mirror Ulua*

"Mirror Ulua"
   Ulua is the general Hawaiian name for the large family of Jacks (*Carangoides*) and Trevallies (*Caranx*). The juveniles of the species *Alectis ciliaris* bear extremely elongated fin spine extensions. The species is also known as threadfin jack, and among some fishermen as mirror ulua due to their very silvery iridescence.

"Mirror Ulua", "Gold and Angelfood", "Aumakua" and many other poems in Part IV utilize some of Jacques Lacan's theories of language function in the unconscious.
   Language is the occasion for the construction of the unconscious, cross referenced in disguises. The semantic ambiguity available in language allows the unconscious to defend the stability of the psyche through camouflage, keeping secret the ideas and feelings experienced at a stage when the mind was unable to withstand the pressure of whatever primary anxiety the early trauma presented. The idea is repressed, and the feeling associated with it is converted into cathexis or relief by substitution into a metaphor that is more acceptable.
   These substitutions are constructed through association, parallels are drawn between the real unconscious idea or desired object, and its symbols, fixations, compulsions, symptoms, goals, meanings, etc. Metaphor, as it were, *releases the original affective charge into cathexis,* and a good deal of the original psychological energy and drive is thereby maintained, though a considerable amount is still bound up in the maintenance of the repression.

In the workings of the unconscious it is "nature's intent" to conceal the most threatening ideas from the unready psyche by "scripting curves of disguise," substituting various forms of defensive metaphors, "encircling the real" trauma "with semblances," *splitting disappointed need into chains of associated desired objects* until such time as the mind is prepared to receive the information defended against.

Desire 'faultily recognized' (disguised in metaphor, displaced onto a different symbol, often by a pathway of sound similarity or physical sensation) is the driver structuring the unconscious by means of its network of associations.

The ambiguity available in language allows the unconscious to keep re-exposing the conscious mind through associations of increasing proximity to the original toxic thoughts, especially in dream images and conscious free associations. Language calls up absent desires, "oblique words that silence or repeat, that evoke and delay," that create hesitations about meanings, mysteriously resonating with the real that has been hidden from consciousness.

We find ourselves pondering phrases and images until they carry us beyond the limits of our memory; this imaginative widening and deepening of attention allows the new reality to enter through sensations and images, through sights, sounds, smells, and touch held in the body's memory. The path through the complex unconscious network of these primary thought records is gradual, protectively hesitant, but becomes the path of connections to the stimulus to which the structures of concealment refer, the path connecting the chain of signifying images (metaphors) leading to the secret of the Other in the history of desire and lack.

Though we desire to know more of our subjective truth, we also fear it. Disclosure of previously defended reality creates newly exposed levels of vulnerability to be mastered. Strategies of beauty, delay, disguise, and proximate vocabulary can ease us past our hesitation, and through the levels of meaning that screen off of the original threat.

It isn't "mimicry" (or metaphor) that uncovers, it disguises. What is uncovered is the unconscious threat or desire that has been heretofore defended against. It is the laws of transformation and disguise that are uncovered, that reveal: "those humbling vulnerabilities, those wilder beauties of my truth," the mysteries of being, finally revealed from the unconscious world.

In similar manner poetry also parallels unconscious structure, especially as described by Lacan. Utilizing those same semantic ambiguities, poems also reveal hesitantly, building the reader's path through a network of associations tangentially related particularly by sound or image to the ultimate statement. Redundancies are selected for their capacity to set in motion resonances connecting chains of signifying metaphors that move toward the mystery symbolized in the text. Symbol then operates through these semantic resonances in the holes of the discourse. Poetic techniques of interferences, counterpoint, metaphor, metonymy, etc, all serve to draw parallels that lead to the literary goal.

Quotes (italicized) and concepts from: Jacques Lacan, The Seminar XI, trans. Miller and Sheridan, and Jacques Lacan, The Language of the Self, trans. Anthony Wilden

"Salvation Painting"
"Salvation Painting," "Admiral Halsey's Orders," "Father"

  The first two of these three poems refer mainly to the 1944 Leyte Gulf sequences in which Adm. Halsey's Third Fleet was following a common decoy maneuver by Adm. Ozawa to lead them away from Leyte Island, where Adm. Kurita was gathering the main force to attack Adm. Kinkaid's Seventh Fleet of troop transports guarding the crucial US supply station. Bill's father was on a Seventh Fleet troop transport, the *USS Anderson*; my father was on a Third Fleet tanker, the *USS Neches*.

  Halsey's maverick move of taking almost the entire Third Fleet north (leaving San Bernardino Strait unguarded) was rationalized by hopes of heroically destroying what he assumed would be the bulk of the Imperial Navy, nearly the whole carrier force, including the two largest battleships the world would ever have seen, just launched as the last hopes of the Emperor after losing most of his air power at Midway. Ozawa's successful diversion of the US Third Fleet left the main population of US troops in extraordinary danger with very few actual fighting ships to defend their fleet. Admiral Nimitz, after many telegraphs attempting to locate the US Navy's main force, sent a final message in which the code reply's inadvertent addendum has become a memorable anecdote of WWII history, "The world wonders." Likely some junior officer had attached the phrase reflecting Tennyson's poem, "The Charge of the Light Brigade." Though an enraged Halsey finally reversed his northward course and steamed south toward Leyte, the endangered US troops were actually rescued by a *very, very* strange occurrence. Within an hour of being able to destroy the US position in the Philippines, Adm. Kurita suddenly reversed *his* course approaching Leyte, owing to fatigue and confusion over lack of information about other Imperial and US

fleet conditions.
For accounts of WWII in the Pacific:
C.*Vann Woodward*, <u>*The Battle For Leyte Gulf*</u>
Evan Thomas, <u>*Sea Of Thunder*</u>

"10/14/80 10:15 am"
    Cicadas in CA? The *Tibicinoides mercedita* (Davis) dwells in grasses, according to The Bulletin of the California Insect Survey, vol.2, #3, 1954, UC Press, Berkeley.

"At Starr's Place"
    Lucky us. We had happened upon Art Shapiro, a truly engaging person, the Distinguished Teaching and Advisor Awards winning UC Davis Professor of Evolution and Ecology, who is one of the world's leading lepidopterists.

Part V- *The Eleventh*

"The Eleventh"
    In <u>9/11, The Culture of Commemoration</u>, 2006, David Simpson maintains: We can't just blame terrorism. If successful communicative actions require "symmetrical conditions of *mutual* perspective taking," without which there can only be a "spiral of violence" recursively duplicating and intensifying itself, then an appropriate environment can only be imagined as resulting from "the political taming of an unbounded capitalism" without which "the devastating stratification of world society will remain intractable." Simpson's quotes are from Giovanna Borradori, ed. <u>Philosophy in a Time of Terror: Diagogues with Jürgen Habermas and Jacques Derrida</u>.

    'Decades' Exponential Hatred': The last three and a half decades have produced abundant literature on this subject, perhaps one of the most relevant to this event being Joseph Stiglitz's analysis, <u>Globalization And Its Discontents</u>, and its sequel, <u>Making Globalization Work</u>.

"Too Big To Jail"
    This poem utilizes concepts and italicized quotes from the following: David Wessel, <u>In Fed We Trust</u>; Paul Krugman, <u>Depression Economics</u>; Joseph Stiglitz, <u>Freefall</u>, <u>The Roaring Nineties</u>; Henry Paulson, <u>On The Brink</u>; Michael Lewis, <u>The Big</u>

Short; Felix Salmon in Wired magazine 2-23-09, article on the David X. Li formula; Michael Lind, The Next American Nation; Richard C. Cook, We Hold These Truths. This last book contains the intriguing quest of Edward Kellogg, an intuitive lay economist who "thought and thought" for years, puzzling over how to reform monetary policy to allow the U.S. economy to better serve its population, finally coming up with Labor and Other Capital in 1849 (published posthumously by his daughter in 1875 as A New Monetary System). You can read it online and see that the same ideas have been around for over 150 years. Also, Stiglitz's latest work, The Price of Inequality, summarizes his most current views on the crisis which is the subject of this poem.

    The following note is in response to Bob Leet's suggestion that I broaden my poem's perspective to include the government's contributions to the creation of the financial crisis. The poem already contained some references to Congressional legislative actions, as well as executive and administrative policies which allowed for the preconditions of depression. Upon some of these factors I have increased emphasis, and also placed a few more references into the body of the poem itself.

    During the 1970s deregulation was extended from common carriers and public utilities to banking, as non-banks were permitted to offer close substitutes for banking services, but without such constraints on safety as were required of traditional commercial banks (reserves levels, investment restrictions, etc). Since these 'shadow banks' were allowed to make much riskier investments with their customers' deposits, they were able to offer higher interest. Eventually the regulations on commercial banks were also relaxed somewhat, drawing them into higher debt to equity ratios in order to compete.

    Bob also brought to my attention the argument that even more influential than these changes in reserves requirements were the shifts in risk management policies that came about once the investment banks became public companies, rather than privately held partnerships. At that point, the incentives for managing risk were replaced by "an overwhelming focus on ever larger bonuses"– (In the June 2012 The Atlantic magazine, William D. Cohan offers a history of economists' considerations regarding the importance of the SEC's 2004 rule change affecting capital reserve/leverage allowances.)

    Also in the 1970s, securitization was created by the US Govt National Mortgage Assoc (Ginnie Mae) to allow packaging mortgages, intended to disperse risk by selling securities to institutional investors and pension funds, thereby also raising more capital to make lower cost loans available for affordable housing. By the 1980s these usages spread to consumer loans, and were more aggressively marketed to global investors. Once the large financial companies (non-banks) were allowed into this market, their increasing complexity created opaqueness, greatly discouraging regulatory oversight.

Governmental administrative attitudes of passivity toward regulation became more widespread, as most obviously demonstrated by the SEC, for example. The structure of regulatory authority was fragmented, being spread over many federal and state agencies lacking inter-agency communication, coordination of information analysis, and often even competing with one another.

The Federal Reserve and Treasury Department had not developed contingency plans for breakdown conditions, and were not heeding warning signs articulated by quite a number of professional economists and government agency officials. (Such as Roubini's concerns about the credit system's fragility; or others' warnings regarding such issues as reduction in personal savings levels; or Brooksley Born's request as Chair of the Commodities Futures Trading Commission to bring securitization derivatives under regulation after the fall of LTCM, a hedge fund.

Beginning in the early 2000s the Federal Reserve's continued loose monetary policy of low interest rates encouraged easy credit, and the administration's 'Ownership Society' policy demanded that banks begin loaning into formerly blue-lined neighborhoods, encouraging vigorous sub-prime lending programs.

Also beginning in the early 2000s, the government began substantially increasing the federal deficit by greatly increased federal spending (mostly defense) while at the same time maintaining substantially lowered taxes.